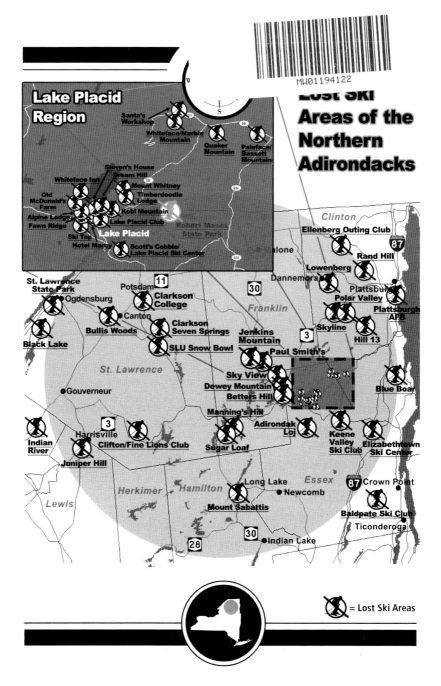

Lost Ski Areas of the Northern Adirondacks

Lake Placid Region

Santa's Workshop · Whiteface/Marble Mountain · Quaker Mountain · Paleface/Bassett Mountain · Steven's House · Dream Hill · Whiteface Inn · Mount Whitney · Timberdoodle Lodge · Old McDonald's Farm · Kobi Mountain · Alpine Lodge · Fawn Ridge · Lake Placid Club · Ski Tor · Hotel Marcy · Lake Placid · Scott's Cobble/Lake Placid Ski Center

Clinton · Ellenberg Outing Club · Rand Hill · Lowenberg · Dannemora · Plattsburg · Polar Valley · Plattsburgh AFB · Malone · Skyline · Hill 13

St. Lawrence State Park · Ogdensburg · Potsdam · Clarkson College · Franklin · Canton · Clarkson Seven Springs · Bullis Woods · SLU Snow Bowl · Jenkins Mountain · Paul Smith's · Black Lake · St. Lawrence · Sky View · Dewey Mountain · Betters Hill · Blue Boar · Gouverneur · Manning's Hill · Adirondak Loj · Keene Valley Ski Club · Elizabethtown Ski Center · Indian River · Harrisville · Clifton/Fine Lions Club · Sugar Loaf · Juniper Hill · Herkimer · Hamilton · Long Lake · Essex · Crown Point · Newcomb · Lewis · Mount Sabattis · Baldpate Ski Club · Ticonderoga · Indian Lake

= Lost Ski Areas

The northern Adirondacks region is home to forty-seven downhill ski areas that are no longer in operation, from small community ski areas to all-inclusive resorts. Many played important roles in the development of the sport on a regional and even national basis. Although most are either fading from memory or into the surrounding landscapes, their stories live on in this book. This map shows the approximate location of these historical places. *Courtesy of Brandon Capasso.*

LOST SKI AREAS

=== of the ===

Northern
Adirondacks

JEREMY K. DAVIS

THE
History
PRESS

Published by The History Press
Charleston, SC 29403
www.historypress.net

Cover: The cover images are courtesy of the Adirondack Museum, Diana Friedlander, the Lake Placid Library—Mary MacKenzie Collection, the New England Ski Museum and the Special Collections—St. Lawrence University Libraries, Canton, New York.

First published 2014

Manufactured in the United States

ISBN 978.1.62619.149.5

Library of Congress CIP data applied for.

This book is dedicated to everybody who played an integral role in promoting alpine skiing as a sport across the northern Adirondacks—including dedicated ski area founders and families, legendary ski instructors, hardworking ski patrollers, passionate volunteers and staff, supportive community leaders and, of course, enthusiastic skiers themselves. Their impacts continue to this day, across the northern Adirondacks and far beyond.

Contents

Acknowledgements

L *ost Ski Areas of the Northern Adirondacks* would not have been possible without the strong support of many passionate skiers, community members and historians who took time out of their busy lives to assist with this book. They took time to find historic photos, explore lost areas and recall their memories—all helping to bring these lost ski areas back to life.

The following people have my appreciation for allowing the use of, as well as sending in, historical imagery—Gerald Abbott, Jeff Allott, Woodward Bousquet, Scott Cahill, William Dolback, Jim Frenette, Diana Friedlander, Roger Friedman, Bob Harsh, Natalie Leduc, Kevin Papenfuss, Laurie Puliafico, Ken Ross, Lyman Ross, Andrew Sajor, William Stevenson, Adam Terko, Ella Tyrrell, Abbie Verner, Ernie Williams and Ross Young.

The following organizations are thanked for allowing the use of materials: Adirondack Museum, Big Tupper, Clarkson University Archives, Goff-Nelson Memorial Library, Lake Placid Library—Mary MacKenzie Collection, Mirror Lake Inn and Spa Archives, New England Ski Museum, St. Lawrence University Library Archives, Town of Diana Museum, Town of Long Lake Archives and the Tupper Lake Free Press.

I appreciate Brandon Capasso's work on designing the four ski area maps, which visually show the location of these various areas.

At the Adirondack Museum, Jerry Pepper was gracious in assisting me with research in its extensive library. At St. Lawrence University, Paul Haggett and Adam Terko were of great help in examining its photographs. Mitch Bresett and Michelle Young have my thanks in the use of the libray's archival material.

Adam Terko, Assistant Nordic Ski Coach at St. Lawrence University (SLU), was of great help in several different ways—showing us the base of the Snow Bowl, exploring Seven Springs, providing research materials on St. Lawrence and visiting the Black Lake ski area. His passion for preserving SLU's ski history is of great service to the university.

Beverley Pratt Reid, Lake Placid historian, was of tremendous help proofreading the stories on the various areas in the region and assisting me with research in the Lake Placid Library. Thanks to Karen Peters of the Wilmington Historical Society for providing a recording of an in-depth oral interview with Sid Maxwell about Quaker Mountain—without her and Maxwell's information, the story of that ski area would have been lost. Natalie Leduc, ski historian for Saranac Lake, was extremely helpful with the research of that region—and is someone who has been passionate about preserving ski history for many decades.

Galen Crane, who wrote an article on ghost ski areas for *Adirondack Life* in 1996, was one of the first to encourage me to research this region. He also assisted with proofreading several sections of lost ski areas.

I had an enjoyable time with good friends Betsy Brown, Rob Michael, Mark Neiswender, Kevin Papenfuss and David Storey exploring several of the lost areas in the region.

I am grateful to the following people for taking the time to speak with or e-mail me with background information on many ski areas—Bob Axtell, Jan Couture, Jim Frenette, Jim LaValley, Lyman Ross, Tim Singer, William Stevenson, Jack Swan, Richard Tuthill, C.B. Vaughan, Douglas Wolfe and Ross Young.

Extensive appreciation is given to www.nyshistoricnewspapers.org and to www.fultonhistory.com, which have made publicly available a nearly full record of archived newspapers. This book could not have been written without these wonderful resources.

The History Press has been an excellent publisher to work with over the last seven years. I would like to thank my commissioning editor, Whitney Landis, for her full support of this project. I would also like to thank Dani McGrath for her sales work for this and my previous books. I would also like to thank the other History Press staff who worked on the manuscript: Julie Foster, Jaime Muehl, Natasha Walsh and Katie Stitely.

The Lost Ski Areas series never would have been possible without the strong support of the NELSAP.org and Snowjournal.com communities over the past sixteen years, which helped grow the NELSAP website from a handful of ski areas to over six hundred. Early support of the website from the New England Ski Museum and Glenn Parkinson helped to give the project gravitas, which eventually led to this book.

Finally, I would like to thank my supportive family and friends, who have been patient and encouraging over the last few years. My husband, Scott Drake, deserves my eternal gratitude for his full support, patience and encouragement while I was writing this book—I could not have done it without him. My parents, Ken and Linda Davis; my brother and my sister-in-law, Nathan and Stephanie Davis; and my mother- and father-in-law, Terry and Phil Drake, have always been there as well.

Introduction

The northern Adirondacks have long been an integral part of the fabric of American skiing and winter sports. For over one hundred years, the region has attracted enthusiasts from all over the world to enjoy its winter splendor. The region is so impressive for winter sports that it has hosted the Winter Olympics twice, in 1932 and 1980. Many famous skiers have trained on its famous hills and mountains, and countless others have learned the sport on its snowy slopes.

Yet despite its international reputation, forty-seven ski areas have become lost in the region, for a wide variety of reasons. These areas, many important to the development of the sport, are rapidly fading away from the collective memory of the area. Physically, the areas are disappearing back into forest, further erasing their existence. It is the intent of this book to preserve their history so they will not be forgotten. Proposed ski areas are included to show the reader examples of areas that nearly existed. Restored areas, formerly lost and now open, show a few examples of how an area can reopen. And even with the loss of areas, seven still operate and have their own chapter to encourage all to enjoy them. Lost ski areas are organized by region and then alphabetically by town.

The northern Adirondack region is defined, by the author, for this book as an area from roughly Ticonderoga west to Blue Mountain Lake and the western foothills and north to the Canadian border. Areas of all sizes are included—from very short rope tow slopes to full resorts with multiple lifts. All areas that are now closed but once had any kind of a ski lift are included.

A Brief History of
Ski Area Development

Skiing can be traced back to the northern Adirondacks in the late 1800s, when visitors such as John Booth brought a pair of skis for a demonstration in Saranac Lake. By the 1910s, cross-country skiing was growing in popularity, along with other outdoor winter sports such as snowshoeing. In the 1920s, the Lake Placid Club was offering instruction on its slopes.

In 1932, the third Winter Olympics were held in Lake Placid. The buzz surrounding the international event encouraged locals to take up even more winter sports, including skiing. The Civilian Conservation Corps soon cut downhill ski trails on nearby mountains, though none was yet lift-served.

The first lift-served ski area was developed at the Stevens House Slope, in Lake Placid, in 1937, three years after that lift made its debut in Woodstock, Vermont. A simple affair, it allowed skiers the chance to make far more runs in a day than when they had to trudge back to the top after each run. It was quickly followed by myriad rope tows sprouting up across the region, as local entrepreneurs and municipalities realized that this sport had staying power and tremendous potential for growth.

Various ski clubs were organized in the mid- to late 1930s across northern New York. Taking advantage of the surging interest in skiing, these clubs attracted new members who wanted to associate with other like-minded enthusiasts. Seemingly every town had its own club, many of which constructed their own small ski areas with rope tows.

With all of these new skiers and areas, professional instruction was sought—one can go only so far learning to ski with trial and error. With few qualified American instructors, professional European instructors were brought in.

The most famous and influential of all was Otto Schniebs, who was the first instructor to teach true alpine (downhill) skiing. Born in Germany and employed as a watchmaker, he immigrated to the United States in 1927, working in Massachusetts at the Waltham Watch Company. While in Massachusetts, he demonstrated skiing on Boston Common, instantly attracting attention. He would shortly relocate to Dartmouth College in New Hampshire, where he coached the ski team to several championships. Following a tragic accident involving the death of his daughter in 1936, he would move to the Lake Placid region, where he would remain until his death in 1971. His famous expression, "Skiing is more than a sport, it is a way of life" was an axiom that all skiers feel to this day.

Otto Schniebs was perhaps the most influential person in the early development of downhill skiing in the northern Adirondacks. His American Ski School taught the sport to thousands. His lectures throughout the Adirondacks increased enthusiasm for the sport. His successful coaching career at Saint Lawrence University brought international recognition to its program. Schniebs also designed several ski areas and consulted with others on their development. *Courtesy of the New England Ski Museum.*

After moving to Lake Placid, Schniebs immediately formed the American Ski School—a group of ski instructors, led by him, that taught skiing with the Arlberg technique on various slopes and areas in the northern Adirondacks in the 1930s and '40s. Schniebs and his instructors worked at nearly every ski area, large and small, and were instrumental in stoking enthusiasm for the sport. Ski clubs invited him to lecture at their meetings, and some areas even held "Otto Schniebs Day" to honor him. He was a rock star in the industry, and everybody wanted the chance to meet him.

World War II would interrupt the development of skiing in the region but did not stop it. Despite many young men leaving the area to serve in the Armed Forces, some ski areas continued to operate—receiving special permission as "physical training centers." While some areas closed for good during this time, others emerged at the end of the war in a position to thrive.

Immediately following the war, more areas opened, and existing ones were improved. Tenth Mountain Division Ski Troops returned to operate areas, instruct at them or work on the ski patrol. Interest continued to grow, and by the late 1940s, the need for larger ski areas became apparent. The northern Adirondacks were being usurped by New England, which was developing much larger centers with more vertical drops than any of the northern Adirondack areas.

The first large-scale ski area was developed on Marble Mountain in 1949. Operated by the State of New York, this area featured a vertical drop in excess of two thousand feet, multiple lifts and numerous trails. The trails were designed by none other than Otto Schniebs, along with another famous skimeister, Hannes Schneider. It had tremendous potential, but high winds scoured away snow faster than it could be replaced, and it was eventually replaced by the new Whiteface on the other side of the ridge. Despite its failure, it gave rise to the idea that the northern Adirondacks could indeed be a major skiing region.

Throughout the 1950s, many areas invested in improved lifts, such as T-bars and Pomalifts, to replace the difficult-to-ride rope tows. Snow packers also became available, allowing for better snow conditions. Hotels and inns opened up their own beginner ski areas on their properties, allowing guests the chance to learn the sport a short distance from their rooms. Even snowmaking, considered by many to be completely unnecessary in the cold environs of the Adirondacks, made its first appearance at the Mirror Lake Inn in 1952.

The height of operational ski areas in the northern Adirondacks occurred from the 1960s until the early 1970s. During this time, areas continued to improve lifts, add trails, expand ski schools and add snowmaking. Many new areas opened during this time, backed by those with strong financial backgrounds. Community ski areas were thriving, bringing new generations into the sport.

By the mid-1970s, a series of events had transpired to decimate the number of operational areas. Larger areas increased competition and provided experiences that could not be matched at smaller areas. A series of poor snow years severely limited the number of operational days, and without snowmaking, smaller areas could not operate. Rope tows and other surface lifts became obsolete, and most areas could not afford to install modern chairlifts. Community-owned areas began to face daunting deficits and were subsequently shut down. Energy price shocks from gasoline shortages developed, and skiers were limited in driving to their favorite areas. Even the growth of other recreational opportunities, such as far-flung vacation spots, became more readily available, diverting attention from local ski areas. The 1980 Winter Olympics, which many hoped would bring in loads of skiers, failed to do so because of a nearly snowless winter.

So many communities were hit hard by the loss of their areas. Most were never profit-makers but, instead, were community gathering places and a place to get some exercise in the winter. A few of the lost areas in this book struggled throughout the 1980s and 1990s, and by 2014, only seven were left in existence.

VISITING LOST AREAS

Every lost ski area section in this book contains information on the potential to visit the area. Some former ski areas are easily accessible and have remnants to view. Others have become overgrown, are difficult to locate or have been redeveloped. Still others are on private property and cannot be visited for any reason. When exploring any of the accessible areas, be sure to keep an eye out for any No Trespassing signs, and always respect the property owners. For the areas described as being on private property, please do not try to explore the area or seek permission to do so.

The author recommends Kobl Mountain, Lowenberg, Mount Sabattis and Whiteface Mountain (Marble Mountain) as the best areas to explore.

I

Lost Ski Areas
of the Lake Placid and
High Peaks Regions

It may seem hard to believe but, at one time or another, the immediate Lake Placid region has been home to fourteen former alpine ski areas, including many that circled Mirror Lake. While most of the areas were served by short rope tows, others—like Kobl Mountain and Mount Whitney—were much more substantial, with multiple lifts, lodges and challenging trails and slopes.

Skiing in the immediate Lake Placid vicinity can be traced back to the Lake Placid Club, a private social organization that was founded by Melvil Dewey, the developer of the Dewey Decimal System. In the 1910s and 1920s, the members enjoyed the club's winter sports programs, which included basic ski lessons. Dewey's son Godfrey would go on to help bring the Winter Olympics to Lake Placid in 1932. The club, while controversial due to its exclusionary membership practices, did put Lake Placid on the map for winter sports.

The region received a huge boost in interest immediately following the 1932 Winter Olympics. This was the first time that the Winter Olympics were held in America, and Lake Placid did not disappoint. Although there were no alpine racing events (those would be added in future Olympics), the general excitement of hosting the event was enough to provide the impetus for developing the region into a ski center a few years later. Otto Schniebs would arrive in Lake Placid in 1936, quickly opening his American Ski School, which trained instructors in the Arlberg technique. These instructors would fan out across the Adirondacks at various areas and teach many the sport.

The first lift-served ski area in the northern Adirondacks was developed on the Stevens House Slope, in the village of Lake Placid, in 1937, and was an immediate hit. It was followed shortly afterward by a private rope tow at the Lake Placid Club. Both were simple slopes, and the desire to have a larger ski center grew. Trails were cut across the High Peaks, such as the Wright's Peak Trail and the Whale's Tail Trail (near Adirondack Loj), but these were not lift-served.

The solution was to build Scott's Cobble, a steeper and larger rope tow area located in North Elba. The idea to develop the ski area was formulated through the Town of North Elba, along with the Lake Placid Ski Club (which still exists to this day, focusing on teaching children to ski). Fred Pabst's Ski Tow Incorporated, the first multi–ski area corporation in the country, leased the area itself. The area offered a much-needed slalom slope and would eventually grow to over three hundred vertical feet with a Pomalift. In the early 1970s, it closed due to tough economic conditions.

Other areas soon followed, such as Fawn Ridge, which would operate for nearly forty years, along with smaller rope tow areas, like Ski Top. World War II temporarily halted skiing at some of these areas, but some were able to stay open during the war. The efforts of skiers like Ron MacKenzie, known as "Mr. Ski" and someone who was instrumental in bringing the Winter Olympics back to the region in 1980, helped keep the rope tow areas staffed with ski patrol during the war. Those that made it through those difficult years were able to grow in the 1940s. One former non-lift-served area, Mount Whitney, had been developed into a more significant T-bar area by the late 1940s.

While used extensively at other ski centers in North Creek, New York; the Berkshires; North Conway, New Hampshire; and in Vermont, snow trains were used only sporadically in the Lake Placid region in the late 1930s and early 1940s. By train, the trip was long—travelers left New York City on a Friday evening and didn't arrive until the next morning—as opposed to trips of just a few hours to closer areas.

During the 1940s and 1950s, various hotels around Lake Placid, including the Mirror Lake Inn, Hotel Marcy and Alpine Lodge, opened up their own beginner rope tows for guests. To help cover the slopes when natural snowfall was lacking, the Mirror Lake Inn even installed a snowmaking machine, well ahead of its time, in 1952.

Still, the immediate area was lacking a major ski area. One was attempted at Kobl Mountain in the late 1950s, complete with a chairlift and expert terrain, but it quickly faltered due to competition from developing Whiteface

Mountain, to the north, and the cost of its own development. Plans to open one at Mount McKenzie never got off the drawing board. Improvements were made at existing areas like Fawn Ridge and Scott's Cobble in the late 1950s and into the early 1970s in an attempt to modernize but were not successful. Most of the immediate Lake Placid areas were closed by the end of the 1970s. Only Mount Whitney was able to stay open into the 1990s, closing after two attempts to resuscitate it failed.

Today, there are no operating areas in the immediate Lake Placid vicinity, though skiers do not have to drive too far to ski at Mount Pisgah in Saranac Lake or at Whiteface in Wilmington. While all of the Lake Placid ski areas are now closed, the area is a major winter sports destination, with Olympic-level facilities in very active use.

Alpine Lodge

Lake Placid, New York

1948–1968

The Alpine Lodge ski area was one of the many Lake Placid hotels that offered lift-served skiing, primarily for guests, and was located three-tenths of a mile from the Fawn Ridge Ski Area. It featured its own ski school, with a dedicated instructor on mostly easy terrain. Despite its small size, several famous skiers and jumpers worked at the ski area and helped give it prominence. Lasting for twenty years, the ski area ceased to operate once the Alpine Lodge itself was closed and torn down.

In the fall of 1948, the owner of Alpine Lodge (formerly known as the Fawn Ridge Club), E. Gardner Prime, decided to open a ski area on its premises, no doubt seeing the growth of other local ski areas. A 450-foot-long rope tow was installed on an 800-foot-wide pasture slope on the northeast side of the property. In addition, a narrow expert trail was cleared in the woods to provide another option for more experienced skiers. William Bowman was hired to manage the ski area, and Inga Prime, a well-regarded Swedish instructor, managed the ski school. While primarily for guests, local residents could purchase a season pass to ski at Alpine Lodge. The lodge advertised heavily to the youth market, adopting the slogan "Where Young People Stay in Lake Placid."

After the first season, "Mezzy" Barber, a nationally known ski jumper was hired to manage the ski center, while Prime stayed on running the ski school. Barber also taught students various skills for alpine and Nordic events. That same season, Barber became the first American ski jumper to jump for 305 feet while at the Rocky Mountain Ski Association Championship in Steamboat Springs, Colorado. Surely, the Alpine Lodge had a well-accomplished manager, and his name recognition brought even more skiers to enjoy the area. Barber also ran the adjacent golf course in the warmer months.

In August 1951, Prime sold the property to Mr. and Mrs. Bruno Wiedermann from Long Island, as he wished to return to practicing law in Lake Placid. Sadly, Bruno Wiedermann tragically passed away a few months later. The area was then sold to Rudolph Davis, who also tragically passed away in March 1957. Despite these tragedies, it is believed that the ski area operated most, if not all, winters in the 1950s. The area was sold for a third time in 1958 to David and Ann Wiseman, who made improvements to the eighty-guest lodge.

Alpine Lodge and the ski area continued to operate through the 1960s, though its use was diminishing as other nearby ski areas grew. In 1967, Nettie Marie Jones purchased the property, and the ski area operated until the early spring of 1968. Jones, the widow of W. Alton Jones, the former chairman of the board of the Cities Service Company, donated the property to become the W. Alton Jones Cell Science Center, a research facility. The W. Alton Jones Foundation would contribute $2.5 million toward its construction. A groundbreaking was held on August 31, 1968, for the center, with the Alpine Lodge itself torn down in early October. The former ski slopes were mostly not touched in the construction of the center, however, a parking lot was built on the upper portions of the ski area. Over time, the slopes have become reforested. The center was open for decades conducting important research but is now vacant.

Visiting the Area

There is currently no public access to the former site of the Alpine Lodge rope tow area. Various satellite imagery shows that the ski area is now woods, and it is highly unlikely that any significant remnants remain of this area.

Dream Hill at Mirror Lake Inn

Lake Placid, New York

1945–1971

Dream Hill, a beginner ski slope located at the Mirror Lake Inn, was a pioneering center, ahead of its time. Besides offering free skiing and instruction to its guests, the area was the first in the northern Adirondacks to feature snowmaking—and remained one of the only ski areas with snowmaking for nearly a decade. The shift of skiing from small hotel or community areas to larger resorts led to its closure as a ski area in 1969.

Throughout the 1930s and 1940s (excluding World War II, when it was mostly closed), the Mirror Lake Inn was an all-inclusive resort in both winter and summer. In winter, it served as a hub for skiers who were discovering the Lake Placid region. It offered ice skating and a toboggan slide on-site.

In the fall of 1945, following the war, Mirror Lake Inn purchased and installed a four-hundred-foot-long gasoline rope tow on its Dream Hill slope, adjacent to the inn. In its first few seasons, the tow would operate for guests during the morning hours and the general public during the afternoon. The tow was also portable and would, occasionally, be brought to the Whiteface Inn if snow conditions were a little thin in Lake Placid. That gasoline tow would run until February 1951, when it was replaced with an all-electric version, though the gasoline tow would remain in the inn's possession and could be moved to the Whiteface Inn if needed.

Any concerns about a lack of snow would be short-lived, however, as manager Jack Wikoff purchased the first snowmaking machine in the area in 1952. Containing sixteen nozzles, the machine could "cover 21,000 square feet of land with an inch of snow per hour." Being a relative easy, smooth slope, only a few inches of dense, man-made snow were required to open the area. Wikoff even advertised that the machine could be rented out around Lake Placid to help ensure snowfall when Mother Nature would not cooperate. Wikoff would joke that every time they would start up the machine due to a lack of snow, they would end up getting a significant snowstorm. Art Adams, who served in the Tenth Mountain Division troops in World War II, was hired to be the area's "Chef de Snow," alluding to the fact that snowmaking is both an art and a science.

On Dream Hill, skiers could learn the sport on an easy, gentle slope. The rope tow is just visible in the background. The proximity to lodging at the Mirror Lake Inn made this area especially convenient to guests. *From the Mirror Lake Inn and Spa Archives, courtesy of Bridget Blinn.*

Opposite: A circa 1950 brochure touted the complimentary ski lessons for guests, provided by a dedicated instructor. Also advertised is the newly opened Whiteface Mountain, later known as Marble Mountain, available a short distance away by car, for more experienced skiers. Note the proximity of the slope to the inn. Here, skiers meet for the ski school at the bottom of the slope.

Throughout the 1950s, Wikoff also taught lessons at the inn. His Jack Wikoff Parallel Ski School was also using methods ahead of its time. The ability for guests to learn on their own uncrowded slope, away from hotshot skiers, allowed many to pick up the sport quickly.

A 1957 letter from owner Mrs. C.M. Wikoff to a prospective guest extolled the benefits of staying and skiing at the Mirror Lake Inn. Take a moment to imagine what it must have been like to enjoy this area in the 1950s.

> *Dear Snow Friend:*
> *When you are with us this winter, and come in from the crisp and bracing outdoors, you'll enjoy not only the cheery indoor warmth of the comfortable inn, but also, the pleasant warmth of the cordial, homelike, informal*

atmosphere typical of this spot, which many of our guests say is a "second home" to them.

Brush the snow from your ski boots, rack up your skis and poles, or hang up your skates, and sink into a deep and comfortable chair before one of the open fireplaces in our game room or lounge, and enjoy the tea and hot chocolate we serve every afternoon.

Then you and your friends can relive the exploits and enjoyments of the day. Maybe you skied on sunny "Dream Hill" beside the inn, where you rode the free tow and benefitted by the lesson that our instructor gives daily to every guest without charge…

…On our "Dream Hill," we have just installed a new-snowmaking machine. Its twelve blizzard nozzles will make sure that there's always snow for your skiing. Together with the indoor ice, at the Olympic Arena, this will insure [sic] a wonderful winter vacation.

The Dream Hill slope continued to operate into the 1960s and found itself as Lake Placid's last remaining hotel ski area for the 1968–69 season. It operated for a few more years until around 1971, when the tow ceased to operate. Skier's tastes were changing, and the days of a learn-to-ski center at an inn or hotel had come to a close.

Visiting the Area

The Mirror Lake Inn and Spa is one of Lake Placid's premier inclusive resorts and welcomes guests year round, including hosts of skiers in the wintertime. The former Dream Hill ski area is now the site of the Mountainview Building, which features views of the lake and surrounding mountains. A small portion of the ski slope remains as a lawn that leads to a cascading waterfall and garden. For more information on the inn, please visit www.mirrorlakeinn.com.

Fawn Ridge

Lake Placid, New York

1940–1977

One of the earliest and longest-lasting (only Mount Whitney survived longer) ski areas in the Lake Placid area, Fawn Ridge was the perfect ski area for beginners and families looking for an affordable place to learn the sport. Located within walking distance of town, it was convenient for skiers who did not have their own transportation. It featured several wide slopes with scattered trees on a 160-foot vertical drop. Its land, worth more for real estate than skiing, was sold in the late 1970s and developed into a subdivision, a fate not uncommon to many smaller ski areas. Despite its closure, its main ski lift continues to operate to this day at another Adirondack ski area.

Prior to opening as a lift-served ski area, the Fawn Ridge Trail, a novice cross-country run, passed through the area. The ski lift was three miles in length and began behind what is now the 1932 Jack Shea Arena. The hill itself was commonly referred to as the Stevens Pasture and featured wide-open slopes. Its proximity to downtown made it a natural choice to open as a ski area, which would help relieve the reported overcrowded conditions at the Stevens House Tow.

In November 1940, the North Elba Park District began to develop the ski area, leased from the Stevens Realty Company. As the slope was not forested, no significant amount of trees needed to be cleared, though the slopes were graded and smoothed. Benton Ames, a mechanic who also operated the Stevens House Slope, was appointed to build the tow and was subsequently granted concession rights. The tow was built rather quickly and was ready by early December.

Prior to the opening, Fawn Ridge was described as having a one-thousand-foot-long rope tow, which would serve wide-open slopes, with adjacent "forest slalom areas" (gladed skiing), perfect for all levels of skiing. A rustic ski cabin was built at the bottom of the tow, which would allow a convenient spot for skiers to warm up and grab a bite to eat. Local skiers were "ecstatic" about the opening, with some even using the slope before the rope tow opened.

On December 6, 1940, Fawn Ridge officially opened to the public, with a foot of snow on the ground. Additional snow fell throughout the month and providing excellent skiing. The arrival of snow trains in mid-December helped boost visitation as well. On December 21, the ski area was used as a training ground for physical education teachers who were expected to

While the slopes at Fawn Ridge were not difficult, they were wide, which made a great learning experience for beginners. Note the scattered trees, which made the slopes more interesting, as well as the rope tow taking skiers to the top.

teach their pupils the fundamentals of this burgeoning sport. Following the class, Otto Schniebs of the American Ski School gave a lecture on teaching the sport.

Snowfall was lacking by New Years, and in early January, a light snowfall proved to be just what the ski area needed. The North Elba Park District rounded up its men and trucks and hauled loads of snow to the ski area, where it was spread out on the slopes. This time-consuming method of keeping the slopes in good operating condition is quite a contrast from today's modern grooming and snowmaking!

Taking advantage of the new ski area, on January 18, a triangular ski meet featuring Lake Placid, Saranac Lake and Northwood Schools was held at several locations. The slalom event was held at Fawn Ridge, the downhill on the Whitney Run, jumping on the thirty-meter jump at Intervale and a cross-country race on the Whitney section.

One of the unique features of Fawn Ridge in the first season was its interconnectivity to the Ski Top Ski Center, located three-quarters of a mile to the southwest. The touring trail was mostly downhill from Fawn Ridge, which made for easy access.

The first ski season ended successfully in the early spring of 1941, and the area continued to operate in the following years, despite World War II. While gas rationing led to more isolated ski areas closing up shop, the proximity of Fawn Ridge to the residents of Lake Placid meant that a car was not needed to access the area. The war certainly provided challenges, though. Ronald MacKenzie, the leader of the region-wide ski school, reported that nearly all of its members were now in the service, leaving him with few able-bodied members. He enlisted the use of local Boy Scouts to help fill in the gap.

Immediately following World War II, changes to the operation of Fawn Ridge occurred. Clarence Lamb, a veteran, mechanic and former skier at Fawn Ridge (who had broken his leg there in 1941), purchased the ski area from the Stevens Realty Company and the rope tow from Benton Ames. He added an additional rope tow at the northern end of the property, which helped relieve pressure on the main lift. Aside from this lift, no significant improvements were made in his first ten years of ownership.

Fawn Ridge received a special mention at the 1948 Saint Patrick's Ski Ball at the Saint Moritz. Three hundred revelers enjoyed the ball while dancing on themed sections of the dance floor—Fawn Ridge, Scott's Cobble and Stevens House. Ski equipment was raffled off during this event.

Lamb was able to make improvements in the mid- to late 1950s, which helped modernize the ski area, at least for a time. In 1955, a Pomalift was built to replace the main rope tow. This 1,200-foot-long ski lift allowed for a more comfortable ride to the summit and saved many skiers' mittens. In 1958, a new Bombardier packer was purchased, which allowed the snow to be rolled after a storm, helping to pin it to the slope. "Snow bunnies" particularly enjoyed the cozy fireplace and sofas inside and the sundeck outside. The lodge was often rented out for special parties during this period.

Lamb also saw the importance of encouraging young skiers to enjoy the sport. At times of low attendance, he would allow children to use the tow free of charge, during the 1950s and early 1960s. In 1967, Lamb retired from the ski business and sold Fawn Ridge to Dick Center, who planned to improve the ski area. Center had previously worked as a ski instructor at Whiteface and at Mount Whitney. A Thiokol Snow Cat was purchased, allowing for even better grooming than the old packer. A seven-day-a-week operating schedule was announced, as opposed to the old schedule, which operated more sporadically during the week. A summer camping area was added to increase revenue in the off-season.

For the first several years of Center's ownership, Fawn Ridge thrived. However, by the early 1970s, issues that affected many ski areas started

Midway down one of the slopes at Fawn Ridge, two skiers pause to take in the beautiful scenery, including distant Whiteface Mountain, which had not yet been developed as a downhill ski area. Lake Placid can be seen frozen over just below Whiteface.

A large glacial erratic (boulder) provides a unique perspective on the slopes of Fawn Ridge toward Lake Placid, as the rope tow hoists skiers to the summit.

making their inroads. The energy crises of the mid-1970s resulted in fewer tourists visiting Lake Placid. The development of larger resorts in the region resulted in a migration of skiers from smaller areas like Fawn Ridge to larger ones like Whiteface. As other ski areas were investing in snowmaking and new, more modern lifts, an area like Fawn Ridge with a Pomalift and rope tow were becoming obsolete.

Operations at Fawn Ridge gradually wound down during the mid-1970s. Scott's Cobble closed in 1973, and some of the beginner lessons for various groups were moved to Fawn Ridge, as the Fawn Ridge Recreational Ski Program. However, this was not enough to make the ski area profitable again, and it closed at the end of the 1976–77 ski season. In October 1977, the Pomalift was removed. The lodge was put to good use, though, as it was leased out to the NYSARC (a nonprofit organization for the intellectually and developmentally disabled) for training in early 1978.

Although the ski area did not make a significant property, the land it was sitting on was quite valuable. Proposals and planning took place in the late 1970s to develop the area as a housing subdivision, taking advantage of the spectacular views. This was approved in 1980, with gradual development of the ski area for homes in the 1980s and 1990s. Some of the slopes became overgrown while portions were kept clear by homeowners to keep the views open.

Fawn Ridge did have one final contribution to the winter sports industry. In the 1980 Winter Olympics, the base area was used as temporary housing for Olympic volunteers, who lived in trailers scattered around the base lodge. These were removed after the Olympics, and Fawn Ridge ceased to be the great novice ski area it once was.

Although there is no skiing at Fawn Ridge, the Pomalift still operates. In 1977, it was moved to Schroon Lake, where it operated at its ski center until 1988, when it was moved to Gore Mountain. It is now the Bear Cub lift, continuing its long tradition of serving beginner skiers.

Visiting the Area

Fawn Ridge is now a housing development located on Algonquin Drive. Most of the slopes and the base area are now either developed or forest. The lift line for the Pomalift is still mostly clear. As the area is on private property, please do not attempt to explore it.

Hotel Marcy

Lake Placid, New York

1950–1967

Starting in 1950, the Hotel Marcy in downtown Lake Placid began offering skiing for its guests with special learn-to-ski packages. It first used a portable tow that could be set up quickly. Located near the hotel on the Grandview Slopes, it was just a few hundred feet long with a vertical drop of about one hundred feet. For the 1958–59 season, the tow did not operate at the hotel but was instead moved to the beginner slope at the short-lived Kobl Mountain. It returned to the Hotel Marcy once Kobl closed in 1959.

A special celebrity visited the Hotel March in February 1956—Clarabelle the Clown, famous from the Howdy Doody TV show, who was photographed using the ski area.

Like many of the nearby areas, the Hotel Marcy hired well-regarded instructors, including Herman Altenfelder and Toni Steurer, who taught lessons in the 1960s.

After the end of the 1966–67 ski season, management closed the Hotel Marcy area, likely due to changing skiers' habits and their desire to learn at a more substantial facility.

Visiting the Area

The Hotel Marcy is now the Northwoods Inn, which features lodging, dining and shopping. The former ski area was located just down Route 86 on a slope that now leads down from the Crowne Plaza. The slope is still mostly clear, but there is a road (Olympic Drive) and tennis courts on the property.

For more information on the Northwoods Inn, please visit www. northwoodsinn.com

Kobl Mountain

Lake Placid, New York

1958–1959

Kobl Mountain (spelled Kobl instead of Cobble due to Melvil Dewey followers) was one of the briefest yet most groundbreaking ski areas in the entire state of New York. The potential of Kobl Mountain was huge—it was a chairlift ski area just a minute or two from downtown Lake Placid, was easily visible from town and had a mix of terrain for all levels of skiers. Unfortunately, the timing of the development coincided with the opening of the much larger Whiteface Mountain, and along with high debts, Kobl was forced to close after just two seasons. Part of it lives on, however, as a portion of the chairlift still operates fifty-five years after Kobl was abandoned.

During the mid-1950s, in the immediate Lake Placid vicinity, publicly available ski areas like Scott's Cobble and Fawn Ridge were small, overcrowded and geared mostly toward beginners. A search began for a nearby, more challenging mountain that could support a chairlift. Located behind the Northwood School, Kobl Mountain, a popular hill for hiking that was within walking distance of downtown, was the answer.

In order to develop the mountain, a corporation was formed with five directors, each with strong credentials and ties to skiing. According to a stock offering, Dr. Harry C. de Valinger, a practicing physician from New Jersey, was the president. John "Jack" Wikoff of Lake Placid, the secretary, was a successful businessman and was the operations manager of the Mirror Lake Inn, a director of the Lake Placid Chamber of Commerce and the second vice-president and a director of the New York State Winter Sports Council. In addition, he was a ski instructor in the United States Mountain Troops. His main role at Kobl would be the operations and facilities manager.

William J. Halloran, the vice-president, was an engineer from Rhode Island and owned his own construction company. Deo B. Colburn of Lake Placid, the treasurer, was a member of the Lake Placid Club and an officer at several Lake Placid–area businesses. He also owned the land that the ski area would use. Finally, Ronald M. MacKenzie of Lake Placid, a director, was a past director of the United States Eastern Amateur Ski Association, a ski coach and a consultant in ski area design. Each director had purchased ten thousand shares of stock.

John "Jack" Wikoff, one of the developers of Kobl Mountain, was an accomplished skier and businessman. Here, in undated photo, Wikoff demonstrates a ski technique in deep powder snow.

A twenty-year lease was secured with landowner and treasurer Deo B. Colburn in May 1956, and immediately following this, 150,000 shares of stock were issued to raise the approximate $200,000 needed to construct the ski area. Expenses would include the building of a chairlift, roads, a snack bar, a restaurant at the summit, a ski and gift shop and working capital to begin the operation.

The initial plans announced to the public in 1956 were to build a 1,500-foot-long double chairlift that would serve four trails of one-quarter to one-half of a mile in length on a vertical drop of 350 feet. Besides skiing, the chairlift would be available for sightseers in the summer and fall, with a restaurant on the summit. The chairlift was to be the first privately owned chairlift in the state, the only other chairlift being at the state-owned Belleayre, in the Catskills. The directors heavily promoted the plans for the mountain throughout the end of 1956 into early 1957, to drum up support and sell stock.

With enough money secured, work began on the mountain in the summer of 1957. By mid-July, a crew was working on clearing the chairlift and Pomalift lines, creating a parking lot and clearing an access road. Five trails and three slopes were cleared. Open slopes featured "tree islands," which created more interesting terrain, and these were touted as providing an "above-timberline experience" because the terrain was more reminiscent of skiing in the West. One of the new expert trails had a thirty-five-degree pitch and dropped off the north side of the mountain from the summit, along with a few other trails. From the midstation of the double chairlift on down, two intermediate and two beginner trails snaked their way to the base of the chairlift and back to the base of what would be the Pomalift, around a beginner slope that was isolated to avoid having hotshot skiers scare away the novices. The Pomalift slope was built to be broad and smooth for beginner skiers, and the lift itself would allow expert skiers an option to return back to the chairlift as it interchanged near the midstation. All of these options allowed skiers of all abilities the chance to fully enjoy the ski area.

Contractors Robbins and White, who had built several ski lifts in New England, were hired to build the ski lifts. With winter approaching, the pace of the installation quickened, and by the end of November, all of the twelve double chairlift towers had been hoisted into place. Most difficult was tower number three, which was thirty feet tall. Pomalift construction was finished in early December, and lights were installed on a few of the trails as well. A basic warming hut near the chairlift was also finished, scaled down from original plans. Kobl Mountain was now ready to open for business—once the snow arrived.

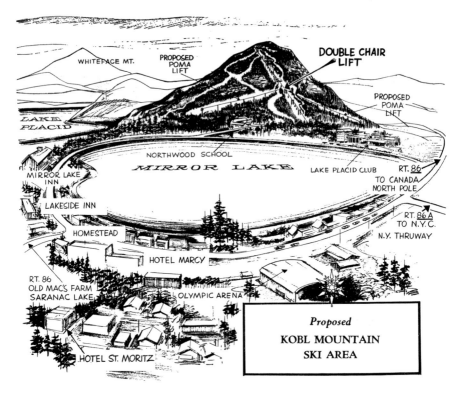

The initial plans for Kobl Mountain show the double chairlift and two Pomalifts, though only the one on the left was actually constructed. Nearby businesses and hotels were marked on the plans to help sell the project's proximity to downtown Lake Placid. *Courtesy of the Lake Placid Library, Mary MacKenzie Collection.*

As it turned out, Mother Nature had other plans. Snowfall in December was sparse across the Adirondacks, which prevented the planned December opening. Barely enough snow had fallen by January 2, 1958, but the ski area finally opened. Temperatures were frigid, near zero, and snow cover was thin. More people came just to ride the chairlift and to see Lake Placid from a unique perspective than to actually ski.

More substantial snow finally arrived by the end of January, and Kobl was open all the way into April and reported a successful first season of skiing, despite the rocky start. In late May, the double chairlift was open for sightseers, who were able to buy boxed lunches and enjoy the picnic grove at the summit. The lift was open until 9:00 p.m., allowing visitors the chance to see the setting sun behind the surrounding Adirondack peaks.

A promotional poster for Kobl Mountain advertises "Skiing for Everyone" and shows the ski area's trails looming over Mirror Lake. The double chair and Pomalift were also advertised. *Courtesy of Diana Friedlander.*

Kobl's double chairlift was the first privately owned chairlift in New York State. This 1958 photo was included in a New York State guide to ski areas and shows the lift rising above Lake Placid. Note that the father is smoking a pipe.

Unfortunately for Kobl, nearby and also brand-new Whiteface Mountain also opened its new double chairlifts that same summer, which, when combined together, provided the longest lift ride in the East, with even more expansive views. Even with this competition, many tourists flocked to Kobl due its proximity to downtown Lake Placid.

Seeking to improve the ski experience, the rope tow that operated at the Mirror Lake Inn was moved to the beginner slope at Kobl in the fall of 1958. This would allow guests a chance to experience a larger ski area as opposed to the novice slope at the inn. Justin Westcott was hired to manage the ski area, and Jack Wikoff took over the operation of the ski school. Opening for its second season on December 20, 1958, Kobl remained open until early springtime.

The increased competition with Whiteface and debts resulting from the $250,000 development of Kobl led to its demise in 1959. The chairlift did not operate for the summer and would never operate at the ski area again. It was a sad ending for a ski area that had the potential to be one that could be enjoyed by all types of skiers, with the convenience of being close to Lake Placid.

On April 21, 1962, the chairlift was sold at an auction to West Mountain Ski Area, located in Queensbury, New York. The chair was dismantled and installed for the following season, where it would serve a wide-open slope, about one-third of the way up West Mountain. A few years later, the chair was heavily modified and expanded to the true summit of West Mountain, where it continues to operate as of 2014, although the only components from Kobl are the lower chairlift towers. The operators of West Mountain, Apex Capital, have made plans to eventually replace this lift, so the last remaining operating feature of Kobl is not likely to be around much longer. It is not known what happened to the Pomalift, whether it was scrapped or sold to another ski area.

As one of the principal developers of the ski area, Jack Wikoff moved on from Kobl and later served as the president of the chamber of commerce, as well as manager of the Alpine Motor Inn.

Visiting the Area

Despite its demise as a ski area, today, Kobl Mountain can still be enjoyed by hikers. It has well-marked trails and features a beautiful view toward Lake Placid. Remnant foundations of the Pomalift and chairlift are still around nearly fifty years after its closure. Portions of the area are on private property, and one should stay on the marked hiking trails.

At the intersection of Mirror Lake Drive and Northwood Road, drive north for about one hundred yards to the new Northwood School access road. There is a dedicated parking area on this access road, about two hundred yards on the left.

From the trailhead, follow the marked trail for about four-tenths of a mile to an intersection. A longer way to the summit, which does not pass by any ski area remnants, heads off to the left. If you want to avoid a scramble on a rock slab, or if the trail/rocks are wet, this would be an easier alternative to the summit. Continuing on the long trail, you begin an ascent up what used to be the Pomalift slope. Portions of this slope are still open, while others have become overgrown. While climbing this section, look to the left—just beyond a row of stones, you can see the lift line for the former Pomalift.

Upon reaching a flat area, the trail turns to climb up a rock ledge. Before doing this, continue walking east a few dozen yards on another trail. With

At the summit, the foundation for one of the chairlift towers remains in good shape after fifty years of abandonment and is now surrounded by forest. Nearby is the counterweight for the chairlift.

some searching, you should be able to see the summit foundations of the old Pomalift. Continuing up to the ledge, footing can be difficult, and a few side trails to the right make the climbing easier.

Once you reach the top of the rock ledge, you are just about at the summit of the ski area. Enjoy the view of Lake Placid and the Olympic ski jumps. This wide-open area was also one of the expert slopes, described as having "above timberline" skiing. A short distance to the north, in the woods, are the foundations and cement counterweight for the lift.

You can return the way you came or locate the long trail at the summit that will take you back to your car.

Lake Placid Club

Lake Placid, New York

1936–1945

The first ski area to be operated by the Lake Placid Club was a rope tow on its property, on the east side of Mirror Lake. It was nearly the first rope tow to open in the region, just after the Stevens House. For the 1936–37 season, a one-thousand-foot-long rope tow was built for the use of members only, as the club and the facilities were not open to the public. The Sno-Birds, a group of skiers within the Lake Placid Club, operated these tows.

Throughout the late 1930s and into the early 1940s, skiing continued on the property, with a second tow being added on the Lake Placid Club Golf Course, where skiers could enjoy smooth slopes. These lifts operated through World War II and were given special permission to obtain gasoline for the rope tow engines, likely as a way to help keep people fit through the war.

In 1945, the United States Army set up a distribution center at the club, and public skiing was no longer available; however, soldiers were able to use the slopes to train and keep in good physical shape. But this was only for their in-town location—the club's Mount Whitney area was soon to develop into a much larger facility and would be the centerpiece of the club's winter sports until 1980.

Visiting the Area

Having ceased to operate seventy years ago, there are no remains of this area. However, the Lake Placid Club Golf Course still operates today and features forty-five holes. For more information, visit www.lakeplacidcp.com.

MOUNT WHITNEY

Lake Placid, New York

Circa 1942–1983, 1989, 1993–1994

The Mount Whitney ski area was one of the longest-lasting of the lost ski areas in the region and was the last of the immediate Lake Placid ski areas to operate. Operated as a lift-served ski area by the Lake Placid Club from 1942 to 1980, the area was first open to only club members and invited guests, ski teams and clubs until 1977. It then became open to the public for a few years before the Lake Placid Club went bankrupt. It closed in 1983. For the 1988–89 season, the Olympic Regional Development Authority (ORDA) reactivated the area to prevent it from losing its permit to operate. This lasted for only one season before the trails and slopes fell silent. One last attempt at operating the area occurred during the 1993–94 season, which would be its last; the base lodge burned to the ground the following year, and the lifts were removed.

Prior to becoming a lift-serviced ski area, Mount Whitney was actively used for downhill and cross-country skiing in the 1920s and 1930s. One intermediate-expert trail in particular, the Mount Whitney Run, was used for racing purposes and was quite thrilling. In the *Ski Trails of New York State* guidebook, this trail was described as follows:

> *The Mount Whitney Run, classed intermediate to expert has been described by Johann B. Thorner, well known Swiss field ski leader of the Lake Placid Club, as follows: "The best time yet made on this run is 1 min. 57 sec. on Dec. 31, 1934. At the very beginning, the skier's skill is tested by an extremely steep descent of about two hundred ft., ending in a sharp curve to the left along a more level stretch, but the speed is still unchecked when the skier unexpectedly comes upon another very steep drop requiring exceptional*

ability to get around a huge tree to the right. This tree is Waterloo to most runners. Here technique and brain work count. The skier who cannot turn when he will, not when the skis will, is lost.

From this notorious tree there is a steady down grade for ½ mile, easily navigated by a medium skier. But the test of the "pudding" comes in the last steep descent with two sharp curves. At this point, the skier gets real speed, and is only able to stand it if that gradual descent above has not weakened his leg muscles so that he can no longer keep control of his skis.

Any skiers heart will beat with joy when he finishes this thrilling run, and it will beat twice as joyously if he has really mastered the difficult parts."

In 1942, the Lake Placid Club installed a rope tow on the Main Slope, which took skiers about halfway to the top. The club was able to obtain gasoline during World War II, which did not interrupt the operation of the area.

Following World War II, the Lake Placid Club planned to enlarge its ski area. With a vertical drop of four hundred feet and moderately steep terrain, the area had potential to become one of the larger ski areas of the 1940s. The first step was to improve access, which was difficult in the 1930s and early 1940s, so the original road was widened, graded and improved, with work starting in 1946 and finishing a year later, in 1947. When finally completed, the road was described as a "boulevard through the forest."

Next on the list of upgrades in the fall of 1946 was a new and modern lift to hoist skiers to the summit. A T-bar, the first in the northern Adirondacks, was ordered from John A. Roebling Son's Company, which was actively building other T-bar lifts across the country. A 1,400-foot-long cut for the new lift was cleared to the summit, parallel to the main slope, which was also extended to the top. Workmen were using a new motor-driven chainsaw that was "equal to the work of twelve men using cross-cut saws." Most of the work was done either by hired workers from the Lake Placid Club, led by foreman Sherry Maynard, or by Sno-Bird Club members.

The steel towers for the lift began to arrive in November, and slowly but surely, the lift towers were erected. The work was quite difficult and unique, as few, if any, of those involved in the construction had ever built a ski lift before. Due to the complexity of the lift and the start of winter, it would not be until early February 1947 that the lift would operate.

Once the lift started hauling skiers to the summit for the first time, any concerns about the long delay instantly vanished. Now, skiers could enjoy a more leisurely ride to the summit, instead of having to grasp a fast-moving piece of rope. More runs were possible in an hour, as the lift had a capacity of eight hundred skiers

Mount Whitney's T-bar transformed the ski area into one of the most modern of its time. Here, two skiers gaze at the lift, which could bring up to eight hundred skiers an hour to the summit. The slope on the left is the lower portion of what became known as the Rock 'N' Roll Slope (cleared in 1948) while the Main Slope is to the right of the lift. *Courtesy of Laurie Puliafico.*

per hour. It truly transformed Mount Whitney from a small, club-operated rope tow area to a private ski area of the highest caliber.

Mount Whitney's T-bar would be unique in the region for only a few years, as a T-bar was built at the original Whiteface a short time afterward. Still, this lift was built to last and served skiers until the area closed for good in 1994.

During the rest of the 1940s and 1950s, the club actively used the area for a multitude of races, college weeks, tournaments and parties. It was the hub of activity for the club in the wintertime. Many members especially looked forward to the Christmas/New Year's period, when activities were at a peak.

Improvements also came to Mount Whitney during this time. In 1948, the Rock 'N' Roll Slope was cleared, providing a solid intermediate route from top to bottom. The slope was completely cleared of any obstacles—so much so that the *New York Herald* stated that "it would take the skill of a phrenologist to detect a bump on this bit of ski terrain."

Ski instruction was always an important feature at Mount Whitney. In the late 1940s, the head of the ski school was Don Traynor, who, in 1950, would go on to become the general manager. In the early 1950s, the club scored a coup when it hired Benno Rybizka, one of the most famous instructors

Mount Whitney hosted many ski races. Here, a skier crosses the finish line on a race held on the Hicks Trail. *Courtesy of the New England Ski Museum.*

of his day, to lead the ski school. Rybizka was second in command of the Hannes Schneider Ski School in Austria. He arrived in the United States in 1936 to head the Carroll Reed Ski School in North Conway, New Hampshire, and was the first in the United States to promote the Arlberg technique, a process where new skiers learn to snowplow and eventually make parallel turns. Rybizka would stay at Mount Whitney through 1953, when he returned to Austria, with Bill Hovey Jr. taking his place.

Hovey was a long-term, well-loved ski instructor. He developed a system of classes that allowed skiers to learn the sport at their own pace, repeating classes if they were having difficulty or moving quickly through them if they were quick learners. By the 1959–60 season, Hovey and his team of instructors were teaching four thousand lessons each year, almost exclusively to members. Tragically, Hovey was killed in a car crash in April 1962, a huge shock to the Lake Placid Club and the region. As a sign of his importance to the area, Hovey later had one of the only four trails and slopes named after him. A memorial race is also held in his honor each year, now held at Whiteface Mountain. Following Hovey's passing, Bruce Fenn took over the ski school.

With the success of the ski school and the overall popularity of Mount Whitney, the facilities need to be expanded further. In 1960, construction began on a new base lodge that was finished in December 1961, featuring panoramic views of the ski area and cafeteria services. A second T-bar, this one 1,600 feet in length, was built on the north side of the hill. The new lift, also ordered from Roebling, helped reduce lift lines on the original T-bar. Both lifts took skiers to nearly the same spot at the summit.

As overcrowded slopes and long lift lines at other ski areas became commonplace in the 1960s and early 1970s, Mount Whitney continued to provide a more spacious ski experience. Brochures from that time contained the slogan "Skiers—in the race for space—you're way out front at Whitney!"

Skier visits declined during the mid-1970s, due to the energy crisis and a shift to larger areas. In order to keep Mount Whitney vibrant and active, the member-only policy was dropped in 1977. Night skiing was also added for the 1977–78 season in order to increase visitation. These actions temporarily boosted attendance but would not last.

Another hit to the area occurred between 1979 and 1980. Despite hopes that skiers would pour into Lake Placid leading up and immediately following the Olympics, this was not to be. A lack of snowfall in those two years, combined with no snowmaking at Mount Whitney, resulted in sparse skiing at best.

Yet another blow hit Mount Whitney in 1980, when the Lake Placid Club declared bankruptcy. The new owner, the Massanutten Corporation, took control of the property and kept it in operation. Longtime-manager Robert Reynolds was kept on staff to manage the ski area.

With the changes in ownership and a lack of recent capital improvements, Mount Whitney was reaching the end of its continuous operation. In 1982,

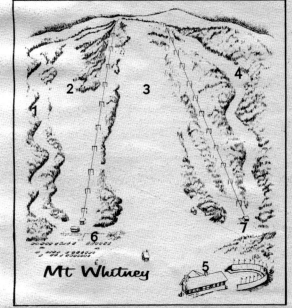

Mt. Whitney Trails

Mt. Whitney now uses the new national marking system to indicate difficulty of trails or slopes. Trail markers are relative to this area only. Look for symbols.

1. HICKS TRAIL — *Easiest*
2. ROCK 'N' ROLL — *More Difficult*
3. MAIN SLOPE (Top) — *Most Difficult*
4. HOVEY TRAIL — *More Difficult*
5. SKI LODGE   6. T-Bar 1   7. T-Bar 2

(Numbers correspond to drawing below)

Mt Whitney

For Your Greater Safety!

Note: Both T-bar lifts at Mt. Whitney comply with new standards of safety demanded of all ski areas by New York State, and meet fully the State's safety code for construction as well as operation.

Mount Whitney featured trails and slopes for all abilities, from the beginner Hicks Trail, to the intermediate Hovey Trail and Rock 'N' Roll slope, to the expert Main Slope. Another trail, "No Name," took skiers from the Main Slope to T-bar number two. Beginners could also take T-bar number one to a halfway unload station to take advantage of easier terrain near the base. *Courtesy of the Lake Placid Library, Mary MacKenzie Collection.*

the Lake Placid Ski Club moved its youth lesson program from the area to Whiteface, which had snowmaking and longer trails. Mount Whitney limped along until 1983 and then closed. Its trails started to fill with brush, and it seemed doubtful that it would ever reopen.

As the permit to operate the ski area in the Adirondack Park was coming to an end, efforts were made to breathe life back into it. ORDA, which operates Whiteface Mountain, entered into an agreement with the new owners of the Lake Placid Club property, the Lake Placid Resort Partnership. Under the agreement, ORDA could invest money into the area only if it was reimbursed. Due to the limited ability to invest in the mountain, only three trails were cleared—Rock 'N' Roll, Hicks and the Main Slope. Only the original T-bar would operate, as there was not enough time or funds to run two lifts. The Hovey Trail was not cleared and would never reopen again. The base lodge was cleaned up, and the area opened again on January 20, 1989, on all natural snow. Mount Whitney operated into March and then closed after an abbreviated season.

The arrangement was not renewed the following year, and once again, Mount Whitney was lost. It would return for one last act during the 1993–94 season. The Lake Placid Land Corporation, which now owned the property, wanted to make sure that the property would be attractive for a possible buyer. Once again, trails were cleared, and the base lodge was fixed up . Pat Cunningham of Cunningham's Ski Barn provided rental equipment, as any skis that were still left in the lodge were outdated.

Mount Whitney reopened on a frigid December 26, 1993, to just a few dozen skiers. For that last season, the area marketed itself as a family-friendly, throwback-type ski area with lift tickets at just fourteen dollars. Manager David Holley worked hard to keep the area open and vibrant under trying circumstances, but despite his efforts, the area would close for good in March 1994.

On May 19, 1995, the base lodge burned to the ground in a suspicious fire, a common fate for many ski areas. So many have had their valuable assets destroyed by arson.

William Grimditch Jr., a part-time resident who had learned to ski at Mount Whitney, led one last effort to form a nonprofit group to buy the ski area and try to reopen it. Noting that it would take a very large sum of money to reopen, he attempted to seek local investors to rescue the mountain. His goal was simple: to have an affordable ski area close to Lake Placid, where skiers of all ages could enjoy the mountain as he had as a child.

But Mount Whitney was too far gone and would not be able to make a comeback this time. In the late 1990s or early 2000s, the lifts were removed, permanently ending any chance of a renewal.

Visiting the Area

The former Mount Whitney ski area is on private property, located a few miles along the private Mount Whitney Road, and cannot be explored. However, the public can clearly see Mount Whitney from the top of the Whiteface Mountain Gondola, especially in the winter. The trails and slopes, once full of skiers, are now becoming filled with trees.

Old McDonald's Farm

Lake Placid, New York

1954–1957

Despite lasting for only a few years, Old McDonald's Farm in Lake Placid was still a significant ski area, with the distinction of having the first Pomalift installed in the northern Adirondacks.

Old McDonald's Farm was a family-oriented tourist attraction that opened in 1953 along Route 86, about one-third of a mile north of the Alpine Lodge. Founded by Julian Reiss, who also owned Santa's Workshop in Wilmington, the area featured a real working farm. Visitors could enjoy everything from hayrides, maple sugaring, dairy operations and square dancing, among many more farm-themed activities. "Old McDonald" himself would roam through the park and visit with families enjoying their visit.

In late 1954, a small ski area was built at the rear of the property, about one-half mile from Route 86, near the Whiteface Club and Resort Golf Course. One of the more modern ski lifts of the time, a Pomalift was constructed as the main lift. Five trails were carved through the hillside for the first part of the season, on a one-hundred-foot vertical drop.

A unique aspect to the skiing was the way it was accessed. While most ski areas feature a parking lot near the bottom of the slopes, this area was more distant. Keeping with the theme, skiers would be transported to the area via hayrides from the main entrance.

In February 1955, toward the end of the season, another slope was ready to open. Seven hundred feet in length, the slope was wider than the other trails. When it opened, a celebration was held, with night skiing and dancing.

The ski area and farm operated until only around 1957. Shortly afterward, Reiss opened up portions of the farm to summer camping for underprivileged city youth, a cause Reiss was passionate about. Two summer camps continue to operate today on the property, as part of the Reiss Foundation.

It is not known what happened to the Pomalift. It was not installed at Fawn Ridge or Scott's Cobble, as they had installed or were installing lifts at the same time that Old McDonald's Farm was in operation.

Visiting the Area

Due to its isolated location and being on private property, the old ski area cannot be explored or visited by the public. To learn more about the Reiss Foundation, which continues Julian Reiss's vision of helping youth, please visit www.reissfoundation.org.

SKI TOP

Lake Placid, New York

1940–1941

A brief ski area that operated for just one season prior to World War II, Ski Top was located at the former Ruisseaumont Golf Course on the Old Military Road. It operated for only one season, from December 1940 until March 1941. Founded by Fred Fortune, Ski Top featured a rope tow and wide-open slopes. A clubhouse served as the hub of the center and offered food service, specializing in homemade soup.

While the area was a bit remote compared to the Stevens House slope and Fawn Ridge, Fortune arranged hayrides to transport skiers from the various downtown hotels to his slope. To add extra revenue, the lodge could be rented out for private parties and meetings.

Some of the last skiing at Ski Top took place on March 15, when the Lake Placid Ski Club hosted a ski jamboree under a full moon. In between ski runs, skiers could enjoy refreshments and card games in the lodge.

Ski Top was probably ready to open for the 1941–42 season, but it is presumed that the outbreak of World War II prevented the opening, and the area closed.

Visiting the Area

Ski Top was located on the Old Military Road, four-tenths of a mile north of the junction of Mill Pond Drive. While parts of the area are still field, the other parts of the old golf course are completely overgrown. There are no known remnants of the ski area.

Stevens House Slope

Lake Placid, New York

1937–1949

The first lift-served skiing at Lake Placid, and indeed in all of the northern Adirondacks, was at the Stevens House Slope. It was an easily accessible lift-served slope, located in the heart of downtown, and was the perfect spot to learn to ski. It operated for nearly a decade, before its demise led to the land being sold. Later, the area was developed for housing.

In the mid-1930s, shortly after the first rope tow began in New York—in North Creek, in 1935—area skiers clamored for uphill transportation. Far more runs could be made per day with some kind of a ski lift as opposed to having to hike back to the top after each run. One such slope that was used as a novice area was on the Stevens House property, in the village of Lake Placid. Aware of the demands for a ski lift, Benton Ames made arrangements with the Stevens House to open a ski area on its property for the 1937–38 season. The tow was constructed in November and December 1937 and opened in the waning days of December. It proved to be an instant hit, as its proximity to town and gentle slopes provided the perfect location to learn the sport. Over the following years, it gained a reputation as an excellent beginner's area.

The slope was the only game in town that was fully open to the public (the Lake Placid Club operated a private tow for guest and members only)

Stevens House Slope was packed with skiers during its first few years of operation. Its wide-open slopes and gentle terrain were the perfect set up for beginners to learn the sport. Here, skiers queue up at the bottom of the rope tow.

The Stevens Hill rope tow began near the shore of Paradox Bay in Lake Placid (note the boathouse in the background). Today, Victor Herbert Road passes through what was the base of the rope tow, and there are no traces of the ski area remaining. *Courtesy of Natalie Leduc.*

through the late 1930s. Special events were arranged at the area, including marshmallow toasts and night skiing. The skiing was fairly simple and did not offer much to expert skiers.

The operator of the tow, Benton Ames, also operated another tow a short distance away at Fawn Ridge beginning in 1940 that provided more vertical slope and helped reduce what were becoming overcrowded conditions. The Fawn Ridge area would gradually gain popularity as the Stevens House Slope slowly waned in the 1940s.

World War II's impact on the Stevens Slope was not as dramatically felt as compared to other areas. Although tourism declined, locals continued to enjoy the slope because it required no driving to access.

The 1948–49 season would be the last at the area. The property was in the process of being sold, and skiing came to an end at the area. Shortly afterward, it was redeveloped for new homes and streets, eliminating any trace of the first lift-served ski area in the region.

Visiting the Area

The Stevens House Slope, located off Stevens Road, is now mostly a residential neighborhood. There are no remnants of the ski area to be found.

TIMBERDOODLE LODGE

Lake Placid, New York

1940s

In the 1940s, the owner of the Timberdoodle Lodge, Fred Schwartz, operated a rope tow for family, guests and friends. It was a simple tow, serving a cleared slope on the lodge's property, and it was not located too far away from Mount Whitney on the Mount Whitney Road. It was never open to the public. The tow likely stopped operating when Schwartz sold the property.

Visiting the Area

Timberdoodle Lodge is still open as a rental property but is on private property and cannot be visited by the public.

WHITEFACE INN

Lake Placid, New York

Mid-1940s–early 1950s

Lift-served skiing at the Whiteface Inn appears to have been a sporadic venture. In late 1944, plans were made to open a rope tow and five slopes at the inn, which would be used primarily for guests. It appears, however, that this development was not built, as there are no contemporary accounts of it operating. Instead, the Mirror Lake Inn would occasionally bring its portable rope tow to a slope at the inn (likely on the golf course) when snow conditions in the village did not permit skiing on its Dream Hill Slope. Once a snowmaker was installed at Dream Hill, the portable tow was not brought to the inn and was likely sold.

Visiting the Area

There are no remnants of this operation, due to the tow being portable. However, the Whiteface Inn is now the Whiteface Club and Resort and offers many amenities, including cross-country skiing. For more information, visit www.whitefaceclubresort.com.

Adirondack Loj Practice Slope

North Elba, New York

1940s–circa 1957

In the late 1930s and early 1940s, the Adirondack Loj, operated then by the Adirondak Loj Corporation and now by the Adirondack Mountain Club, served as a headquarters for downhill and cross-country skiing. It included trails such as the Wright Peak Trail, designed by Otto Schniebs, and the Rimrock Ski Run, off Mount Jo, which featured a thrilling descent. In order for skiers to practice and warm up before tackling these runs, a practice slope was cleared on a hill off the southwest side of Heart Lake. A rope tow was built at some point in the 1940s to allow skiers to make more practice runs in a shorter period of time. The slope itself was simple, 60 to 80 feet in width, with a vertical drop of 150 feet.

In 1957, the tow was sold to the developing Beartown Ski Area near Beekmantown, thus ending lift-served skiing at this slope. However, the slope is still maintained and is available today to those wishing to practice before beginning their backcountry adventures from the Loj. Thus, it is only lost in that the lift is gone and not that the slope is no longer in use.

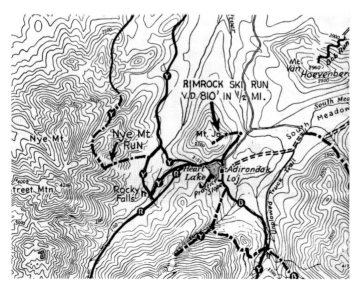

This early 1940s map of the trails around the Adirondack Loj shows the location of the practice slope off the southwest shore of Heart Lake. Also visible on the map is the Rimrock Ski Run, a sporty class C racing trail that had a vertical drop of eight hundred feet but was not lift-served. *Courtesy of the New England Ski Museum.*

Visiting the Area

The slope can be visited by starting from Adirondack Loj and taking the trail around Heart Lake to the southwest corner. The slope connects with this trail and is a short and easy hike to the top. For more information on the Adirondak Loj, please visit www.adk.org.

Scott's Cobble

Lake Placid Ski Center

North Elba, New York

1938–1973

Scott's Cobble—not to be confused with another nearby ski area called Kobl Mountain, which operated in the 1950s—was the Lake Placid region's first significant-sized ski center. While the Stevens House Slope and the Lake Placid Club operated rope tows a year prior to the opening of Scott's Cobble, these were smaller, simpler areas. Scott's Cobble was not only the first to offer a more sustained vertical, a slalom slope and a warming hut, but it was also the first ski area franchise in the northern Adirondacks. It operated for thirty-five years, from the pioneering days of the ski industry to the energy crises of the 1970s.

After the fledgling 1936–37 season, the first to offer lift-served skiing, plans were drawn up by the Lake Placid Ski Club and the Town of North Elba to develop a ski center close to town, preferably on public land. State land could not be developed; however, a parcel was available adjacent to the Lake Placid Golf Course (now the Craig Wood Golf Course), which would be suitable for skiing. It faced north, had a sustained pitch and was not excessively far from town. However, it was not within walking distance, which led to issues at times. Soon it had to compete with closer, but smaller, ski areas in town. The Ski Club made recommendations for slope layout, and clearing of the main slope began on September 22, 1937.

In order to market this new ski area, an "instructor of international recognition" was sought who could lend credence that this would be a serious operation. Otto Schniebs of the American Ski School was brought in. He helped oversee the trail design, and his ski school instructed skiers at the slope. Howard Bentley, a well-regarded naturalized citizen from Switzerland, was hired to teach the majority of classes for the first winter. It was hoped that an instructor like Schniebs would increase the visibility of Scott's Cobble and draw in skiers from far and wide.

The second step was to find an operator and to obtain a ski lift. At this time, Fred Pabst's Ski Tows Incorporated was opening and leasing ski areas throughout the Northeast, Midwest and Canada. Pabst, of the Pabst Brewery family, was well ahead of his time, as ski area conglomerates would really not take off until about fifty years after Scott's Cobble was developed. Pabst's company typically would install a rope tow or a J-bar lift, of its own design, and hire managers and operators for the lift. Discussions with Ski Tows Incorporated engineer Seth Pollard progressed in the fall of 1937, with an original plan to install a 2,400-foot-long J-bar lift. However, this plan was scuttled as time was running short for the upcoming winter, and a rope tow was chosen. Plans were made that a J-bar would still be installed for the following season, but this would not be the case. Pabst himself inspected the area in mid-November 1937, declaring the slope "a natural choice with outstanding possibilities."

As winter approached, time was running out to construct the ski lift. It was completed on January 6, 1938, and the Town of North Elba and the Lake Placid Ski Club planned to host a ski jamboree. Opening on January 7, 1938, Scott's Cobble welcomed the public with a large slalom slope, several trails, a near three-hundred-foot vertical drop and a ski cabin as a warming hut. The slopes were packed, and the area made an immediate impression on all who visited. The positive press reports cited that Scott's Cobble, and all of the other improvements in Lake Placid, would help put the region on every skier's map. The first season was such a hit that the Ski Club promoted spring skiing until the snow melted away.

Over the following two seasons, additional improvements came to Scott's Cobble, including a new trail to the east of the main slalom slope, as well as glade skiing. The ski cabin was moved closer to the ski lift, which gave spectators a chance to watch the skiers from inside the lodge.

Major changes were in store for Ski Tows Incorporated for the 1941–42 season. Pabst ended all of the Ski Tows Incorporated franchises and instead concentrated his energies on the largest mountain he owned, Bromley, near Manchester, Vermont. Some ski lifts were removed from some of his resorts and installed at Bromley, including a J-bar from Cobble Mountain in Lake

An aerial view of Scott's Cobble shows the variety of skiing offered at the area. The base cabin can be seen at the foot of the slope. The rope tow is visible through the trees, with the midstation for beginners about halfway up. Most prominent in the center is the broad slalom slope that was the site of many races. At the edges of the ski area were two trails that provided alternate ways of reaching the base. *Courtesy of the Lake Placid Library, Mary MacKenzie Collection.*

George (yes, there were a lot of "Cobbles" in New York). The tow remained at Scott's Cobble but was moved to the south, and a second section was added. This allowed beginners to use the lower lift while experts could continue on the second stage to the summit.

Unfortunately, these improvements were ill timed. With the advent of World War II, most of the young men who frequented Scott's Cobble were drafted into the war. Gas rationing also affected the area. However, because Scott's Cobble was a municipal ski area, it remained open, on a limited basis, through the war. Its relative distance from Lake Placid made access difficult, compared to Fawn Ridge, which was within walking distance.

After the war, Scott's Cobble regained some of its popularity and was frequently the site of ski races for all ages. Many local schools held

Slalom racing was quite popular at Scott's Cobble, drawing in racers and spectators alike. This view shows skiers waiting at the top of the course on a large rock, along with spectators at the bottom. Note the cliffs near the summit that provided a natural edge for the slope. *By Ernie Williams, courtesy of Natalie Leduc.*

meets at Scott's Cobble, whose wide slalom slope was unmatched in the local vicinity.

In 1955, after nearly twenty years of being a rope-tow ski area, the Town of North Elba appropriated $15,000 (nearly $130,000 in 2014 dollars) to replace the lifts with a more modern Pomalift. Pomas were substantially easier to ride than rope tows and featured a detachable hangar with a rubber disc attached at the bottom on which skiers rode to the summit. It was hard to catch clothing on this lift, which was a problem with rope tows, and nobody's mittens would be chewed up. Skiers welcomed the improvement, which helped Scott's Cobble become a modern ski area.

Just a few years later, nearby Whiteface would open, a ski area with tremendous vertical and terrain—especially compared to a smaller area like Scott's Cobble, despite its recent upgrades. There was discussion that the area should be shut down and that its usefulness was over. Ronald MacKenzie, who had been part of the board of the Lake Placid Ski Club that had urged Scott's Cobble to open in the first place, pleaded with the town to keep the ski area in 1960, stating that it still had a purpose as a training and learning hill. His pleas were heard, and the area remained open.

Few changes occurred at the area until 1967, when Art Jubin and Bill Sullivan leased it from the Town of North Elba and renamed it the Lake Placid Ski Center, hoping that the name change would increase recognition of the area. This lasted only a few years, and in 1969, it reverted back to town management, and the name was changed back to Scott's Cobble.

The draw of Whiteface and other larger mountains continued to drain Scott's Cobble of potential skiers. Its limited terrain and vertical could not compete with the larger developments. The area consistently lost money, nearly $4,000 a year through 1973. This loss could not be sustained, and the town decided that the time for downhill skiing at Scott's Cobble was over.

After its closure, the cabin was removed, as was the lift, and its eventual whereabouts are unknown. The Lake Placid Ski Club moved its ski program to nearby Fawn Ridge for the 1973–74 ski season. Trees and brush quickly took over the slope, and four decades later, the area is hard to detect from a distance. However, several remnants of the area remain.

In 2009, the author and his friend David Storey were given permission to hike and explore the area. The old lift operator's shelter at the base of the Pomalift was near collapse. A rusted folding chair sat alone outside the hut, the lift operator who last sat on it long gone. Climbing uphill, the lift line for the Pomalift was still relatively clear, with occasional foundations still present.

At the top of the Pomalift, the counterweight and supporting tower remained in place in 2009, thirty-five years after the closure of Scott's Cobble. The counterweight provided the appropriate balance for the lift and kept it stable.

Near the summit, the operator's hut was in better shape than the lower one but was not far from collapsing as well. At the top, the counterweight for the lift and associated tower were perhaps the most substantial remnants found.

Returning to the bottom, via the old Slalom Slope, it was striking how overgrown this slope had become. It was hard to believe that what is now forest was once teeming with happy skiers and slalom racers. The side trails are also completely overgrown and unrecognizable. Scott's Cobble is truly gone.

Visiting the Area

Due to its location bordering the active Craig Wood Golf Course, which is owned by the Town of North Elba, hiking and exploring the former Scott's Cobble requires permission from the management. If you would like to see the area, it is best to look at the former slope while enjoying a round of golf, though there is not much to see. From the fifth hole, look east at the forested hillside. It is nearly impossible, however, to make out the exact outline of the former trails, though in winter, you can nearly make it out. Forty years have mostly erased any evidence of the ski area when viewed from a distance.

To learn more about the Craig Wood Golf Course, visit www. craigwoodgolfclub.com.

II

Lost Ski Areas of the Saranac Lake, Tupper Lake and Long Lake Regions

S kiing has been a part of the Saranac Lake region for over 120 years. According to Allen Adler's *New England & Thereabouts—A Ski Tracing*, the first skis are believed to have arrived in the area in 1892. At that time, John R. Booth from Ottawa, Canada, had brought a pair for a demonstration—and local residents quickly wanted to duplicate what they had seen. They had Napoleon Bailey, a local carpenter at Branch and Callahan's Mill, make skis for their own use.

By 1907, skis with basic bindings appeared in store windows, and J. Insley Blair of Tuxedo Park performed an exhibition with a nine-foot-long pair of skis on Slater's Hill. Dr. William Soper brought improved skis—including the latest bindings—to the area. Soon, small ski jumps and occasional cross-country competitions began to appear in the Saranac Lake region. A Saranac Lake Ski Club was formed, and at its annual banquet in 1922, the United States Eastern Amateur Ski Association was formed, which would be instrumental in developing the sport throughout the country.

As interest continued to grow in the 1920s and 1930s, particularly after the 1932 Winter Olympics in nearby Lake Placid, the stage was soon set to develop a downhill ski center. In 1938, the first rope tow in the Saranac Lake region was built on Donnelly's Farm in Harrietstown, serving an open slope. Interest continued to grow, and a few years later, another rope tow was established at Better's Hill, closer to Saranac Lake itself, followed by a tow at Dewey Mountain. In the 1950s, skiing shifted to Mount Pisgah—a larger development with over three hundred feet of vertical—that would expand from a rope tow to a T-bar. It became a community treasure that continues to operate to this day, providing residents and visitors an enjoyable ski experience.

In nearby Tupper Lake, winter sports were also developing during this time. The Tupper Lake Rod and Gun Clubhouse advertised the area to snowshoers from Ottawa, Canada. A snow train full of snowshoers arrived in 1936, and with the success of that trip, Tupper Lake knew it could be a winter sports center. In 1939, its first rope tow was established at Manning's Hill, followed by another, larger development on Sugar Loaf in 1940. These two areas were the impetus for the future Big Tupper development, which was planned in the 1950s and opened in 1960.

Paul Smith's College was one of the few colleges in the country to operate not one but two ski areas—a rope tow on campus and a racing/jumping complex on Jenkins Mountain. While Jenkins Mountain was never built out to its full potential, many of the students who skied and raced there went on to play critical roles in the local ski industry.

Long Lake, also seeking its own ski area in the 1960s, developed one on Mount Sabattis in town, mostly for its own residents. Like many town-owned Adirondack ski areas, it allowed for healthful outdoor recreation during the long, cold winter months.

By the 1980s, all of the rope tow–only ski areas had closed, leaving only Big Tupper and Mount Pisgah to carry on the traditions established nearly a century before. Both have the strong support of their local communities and should continue to provide skiing for a long time to come.

Sky View Ski Center at Donnelly's Farm

Harrietstown, New York

1938–circa 1941 and 1946–1950

The Sky View Ski Center was in operation twice—once before World War II and again after the war. It served a relatively gentle slope with beautiful views on the Martin Donnelly Farm. Once nearby Mount Pisgah opened, skiing began to dwindle, and it closed at the end of the 1949–50 season.

Beginning in 1938, a rope tow operated on the farm, managed by Hector Woods and Charles Keough. Skiers bought tickets at a small booth and skied behind the farmhouse, where they could enjoy the 150-foot vertical. However, the area was fairly far from the village, and other, closer ski areas like Dewey Mountain and Betters Hill were easier to get to. With the outbreak of World War II, Sky View closed.

In 1946, local skiers Joe Perry, along with Curtis and Raymond "Pappy" Wamsganz, wanted to reactivate the ski slope. The old tow had been removed. According to a 1996 *Adirondack Life* article, written by Galen Crane, the men purchased a 1936 Ford V-8 engine to power the new tow and used second-hand telephone towers for the poles. When the lift first ran in December 1946, it went at an eye-popping thirty-five miles an hour but was quickly adjusted to slower speeds. While there were no restrooms, skiers were allowed to use the facilities in the farmhouse, if they took off their shoes.

Operating until 1950, the area was popular but offered limited terrain. Joe Perry taught lessons during the four seasons of operation and taught hundreds the sport. Once Mount Pisgah was opened, skiing ceased at Sky View, and the rope tow was sold to the new area.

Visiting the Area

While the farm itself is a private ski area (and there is not much to see of the slope from the road), explorers can still visit a portion of the ski area. The former ticket booth is now used for Donnelly's Soft Serve Ice Cream—which the author can attest to as being the best of its kind. The ice cream stand operates mostly during the summer months and is well worth a visit.

MOUNT SABATTIS

Long Lake, New York

1960s–1970s

In the 1960s and 1970s, the Town of Long Lake operated a rope tow on its Mount Sabattis Recreation Area. The tow was quite long for a local ski area—nearly 1,700 feet. Two broad slopes were available, each about one-third of a mile long. There was no snowmaking.

The ski area was mainly for town residents and local children and was not marketed to destination skiers. It was used by the local school for physical education classes, along with local Boy Scouts troop, who used the area for their field days.

It is unknown exactly when the area closed, but it was likely around 1980.

Visiting the Area

Mount Sabattis remains a public park and is easily found in Long Lake, at 1100 Deerland Road. The trails are still kept clear, as is the rope tow lift line. From the parking lot next to the tennis courts, follow the road uphill that follows the former rope tow, and in seven hundred feet, you will enter the forest. Continue climbing another seven hundred feet until you reach an open slope. Yet another seven hundred feet ahead will lead to the summit, with beautiful views of Long Lake. You can descend the same way you came up or via one of the ski trails, which are still fairly clear.

Winter sports enthusiasts can still enjoy the recreation area, with public ice-skating and a groomed sledding area.

Although no longer used for alpine skiing, the Mount Sabattis Recreation area is still used for wintertime sports, including sledding and ice-skating. This recent view shows the sledding hill on the left, at the base of a former ski trail, with lights for night use. The old lift line for the rope tow goes up through the woods on the right. *From the Town of Long Lake Archives, courtesy of Abbie Verner.*

JENKINS MOUNTAIN

Paul Smiths, New York

1949–late 1950s

Jenkins Mountain was one of the few ski areas owned and operated by a college or university in the northeastern United States. While it did not reach the same level of prominence as other college areas—such as the Middlebury College Snow Bowl, in New Hampshire, or the St. Lawrence University Snow Bowl—it was still a significant area that contributed to the sport.

In 1949, Paul Smith's College began construction of what was intended to become "the most complete collegiate ski center in the United States." It would be one of the very few ski areas located on campus—though Paul Smith's included twenty thousand acres of nearby land, and the ski area was located over two miles from campus. Work began in September and was mostly completed by students, under the supervision of ski coach Rainbow Wright (a former St. Lawrence University skier), as well as Dr. David McKee. The facilities were quite extensive and included a three-thousand-foot-long downhill run (the lower half was an open slope with scattered tree islands), a twenty-meter ski jump and a forty-meter ski jump.

With over two hundred student volunteers, mostly forestry majors, the area was built in just two months and was finished in November 1949. The new trail, as described in an article in the *Ogdensburg Journal*, "curves down the side of the mountain for 1,800 feet, leading into the inverted-funnel shaped clearing, the slope that extends down the remaining 1,200 feet. The width of the slope spreads out to 250 feet at the bottom…the combination trail and slope is designed for utmost safety as well as for speed." A touring trail was also built to connect the campus with the ski area, along with a one-way dirt road from Route 30. This led to a parking lot for fifteen or twenty cars, according to Bob Axtell.

In addition to the ski slope and trail, a 1,400-foot-long rope tow was installed. This took skiers about halfway to the top and allowed them to make numerous practice runs. It was open to the public for "a nominal fee."

On January 12–14, the fourth annual Paul Smith's Winter Carnival was held, with some events at Jenkins Mountain. Eight ski teams, including Clarkson's and Penn State's, attended. The carnival began with a torchlight parade on the campus ski slope on the twelfth, with the downhill and slalom events held at Jenkins Mountain on the thirteenth. On the fourteenth, a cross-country race was held on the trail to Jenkins Mountain, followed by ski jumping at the area. The event was a success and helped put the area on the map.

On March 11, 1951, the area hosted a United States Eastern Amateur Ski Meet. Bob Axtell, who would later manage the St. Lawrence University Snow Bowl, won the meet, which included a slalom and downhill race, ski jumping and a cross-country race.

Throughout the rest of the early mid-1950s, Jenkins Mountain was used during Winter Carnivals, as a training facility for the ski team and for occasional use by the public. Several state cross-country and downhill competitions were also held at the site.

By the late 1950s, the use of Jenkins Mountain had begun to dwindle, perhaps due to its remote location and the lack of any significant capital improvements. It had closed by 1960 and today is reforested.

Visiting the Area

Jenkins Mountain is accessible from a trail that stems from the Paul Smith's College Visitor Interpretive Center, located off Route 30, just north of campus. Be sure to obtain a trail map from the center or from its website. From the visitor center, follow the Jenkins Mountain Trail west past the intersection with the Long Pond Trail (remaining on the Jenkins Mountain Trail). The next landmark will be a privy on the right. The ski area was located along this trail, about eight hundred feet beyond the privy. As it swings parallel to Jenkins Mountain itself, you can look on the right where the former slope was located, though it is mostly grown in. If you look hard enough, remnants of the rope tow can be found. You can continue on the marked trail to the summit of the mountain (which does not go up to the former ski area) or return to your car.

For more information on the Visitor Interpretative Center, please visit www.adirondackvic.org.

PAUL SMITH'S COLLEGE

Paul Smiths, New York

Circa 1950–circa late 1950s

In addition to their Jenkins Mountain development, Paul Smith's College operated a short rope tow on campus, near Lambert Hall. This tow was available for free to students and to the public, at a rate of $1.50 per day. Only 250 feet in length, the tow served a 50-foot drop and was geared toward beginners. Natalie Leduc remembers that the tow had a button that could start and stop the lift at any time, so students could use the area at their leisure. It was often used for torchlight parades for their Winter Carnivals. It is unknown why the college stopped operating the lift, but its small size and limited terrain likely played a role.

Visiting the Area

As Paul Smith's College is a private institution and there is nothing left of this ski area, please do not attempt to explore it.

BETTERS HILL

Saranac Lake, New York

1940–1941

Betters Hill was the location of the Village of Saranac Lake's first rope tow and was in existence for several years. In the late 1930s, an open slope on Betters Hill was the location for slalom and downhill ski races for the Saranac Lake Winter Carnival. A small ski jump was also in use at this time. Then, in November 1940, Thomas Cantwell purchased a nineteen-year-old village ambulance, whose engine would be used to power a ski tow that he had built on the hill. A crew of workers, mostly recruited from clients of Cantwell's father, Francis, assisted in the construction of the tow. Described as a group of "winos, drifters and ex-cowboys," these workers had been

The Betters Hill ski area featured wide-open slope skiing with panoramic views. This photo shows two skiers at the summit, gazing toward Saranac Lake Village and Mount Baker in the distance. *Courtesy of Natalie Leduc.*

bailed out of trouble by Francis, who was a lawyer, so they were loyal to the family. The tow offered skiers a 150-foot vertical drop and overlooked the northwest edge of Lake Flower, with Baker Mountain visible in the distance.

The ski area operated for only one season. In March 1941, Cantwell volunteered to go into the army for World War II and had to sell the tow. His assistant, Bob Demers, wrapped up the operation for the season. Cantwell had offered the area to the Village of Saranac Lake, but it did not move on his offer, and instead he sold it to St. Lawrence University, which would later install it at its Snow Bowl area.

Visiting the Area

According to ski historian Natalie Leduc, Betters Hill was located a few hundred yards south of the junction of Branch Farm Road and Kiwassa Road. The area is mostly reforested today.

Dewey Mountain

Saranac Lake, New York

1941–1942

Dewey Mountain was very briefly the location of a lift-served ski area. Its location was selected because it was closer to the village than Donnelly's Farm or Betters Hill. In late November 1941, the village authorized $300 to be spent to create a ski slope at Dewey Mountain. Although public money was spent, the tow was operated privately by Guy Wood and Charlie Keough and was one thousand feet in length. It appears to have operated for only the 1941–42 season before World War II put an end to the skiing, and the tow was sold to the village.

Visiting the Area

Although there are no traces of the former ski area, Dewey Mountain is a vibrant recreation center, with mountain biking, hiking, cross-country skiing and snowshoeing. For more information, please visit www.deweymountain.com.

Manning's Hill

Tupper Lake, New York

1939–1940

The idea of expanding winter sports in the Tupper Lake Region started in the early 1930s, when efforts were made to expand the area's offerings outside of the timber industry. With deep snows and varied terrain, Tupper Lake was perfect for a wide variety of sports, including snowshoeing and skiing. Ottawa, Canada, was targeted, and Dr. Glenwood Delisser of the Tupper Lake Rod and Gun Clubhouse convinced snowshoe clubs from Ottawa to visit Tupper Lake.

On the weekend of February 28–29, 1936, the first snow train from Ottawa arrived, bringing 156 snowshoers from eight clubs. This was the first large-scale winter tourism activity in Tupper Lake. In April 1936, a new club, the Pioneer Snow Club, was formed to continue to develop Tupper Lake for winter sports.

In 1939, following the trend of many Adirondack towns, the Pioneer Snow Club (along with the chamber of commerce) scouted out a location for Tupper Lake's first lift-served downhill ski area. They found an open slope behind the Manning home, which would be perfect for a tow and was easily accessible. In the fall of 1939, a rope tow was "cobbled together using a log loader and automobile pulleys," as remembered by then eleven-year-old skier Jim Frenette.

The ski area would operate for only one season, closing in 1940. "It was simply too small and a larger area was needed," recalls Frenette. A new area, which became Sugar Loaf, was developed for the following season, and the short-lived Manning's Hill passed into history. Despite its brief existence, it had introduced skiing to Tupper Lake, which led to Sugar Loaf and, eventually, the development of Big Tupper.

Visiting the Area

Manning's Hill is located on private property, behind the Lakeside Veterinary Clinic at the junction of Lake Simond Road and Route 30. There is little to see, as the slope has returned to Adirondack forest. There are no remnants of the ski area remaining, although in the mid-1990s, Jim Frenette did find several rope tow pulleys, which have since disappeared.

SUGAR LOAF

Tupper Lake, New York

1941–1949 and 1957–1960

Sugar Loaf was the original ski center in Tupper Lake and was the precursor to the much larger Big Tupper Ski Area that opened for the 1960–61 season. It operated in several phases: a few years prior to World War II, then in the postwar growth, then it closed due to a lawsuit and its final four seasons were in the late 1950s. The area was popular with both children and adults and was a main source of winter recreation in town.

In the late 1930s, the Tupper Lake Winter Sports Association decided to develop a ski center, taking advantage of the surge in popularity of lift-served alpine skiing that began at Manning's Hill. A suitable location was scouted on Sugar Loaf Mountain, immediately adjacent to the Tupper Lake Golf Club. The property, owned by the Oval Wood Dish Company (a major employer in town), was generously leased to the club at no cost. Willard J. Wilkinson donated his time to survey the land and determined that it would make an excellent ski area.

In early October 1940, local woodsmen began to clear a slope, and they were joined by dozens of volunteers a few weeks later. The slope was cleared to 120 feet in width and was 800 feet long, with a maximum grade of 21 percent.

The Stump Hill Trail was built to connect the area to the nearby Waukesha Parklands. A Fordson tractor engine powered the rope tow, and the rope itself was strung up in October. A small warming hut, managed by Helen LaValley, was built to provide skiers a location to take a break in between runs and to provide refreshments.

To prepare for the opening, five thousand copies of a trail guide to Sugar Loaf, designed by Howard Hutchins, were sent to the New York Central Railroad and the sporting goods store Abercrombie and Fitch, and the area was advertised on Macy's Ski Map. In addition, the guide was sent to ski clubs and chambers of commerce throughout the state. An opening in December looked promising, and some skiers enjoyed the slopes by hiking to the top and skiing down. However, a period of mild weather and a lack of snow delayed the official opening until January 18.

The official opening was a success, and within weeks, the area was teeming with skiers and those looking to learn the sport. A January 30, 1941 article in the *Tupper Lake Free Press* described the immediate success of the area as

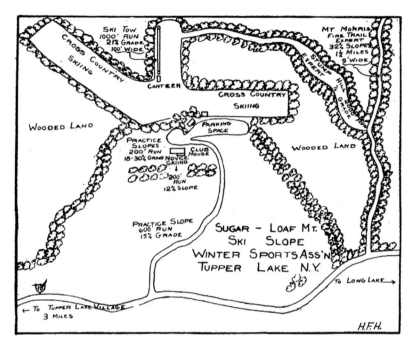

Sugar Loaf's 1941 promotional map, designed by Howard Hutchins, shows the ski tow slope, the expert Stump Hill run and various practice slopes on the golf course. *Courtesy of the* Tupper Lake Free Press.

This January 1941 view of the slope at Sugar Loaf was one of the first taken at the brand-new ski area. From the summit, skiers enjoyed views of the nearby snow-covered golf course and Tupper Lake. The rope tow path is visible on the right. *Courtesy of the* Tupper Lake Free Press/Goff-Nelson Memorial Library.

The rope tow was originally on the left side of the slope as one faced the top. This early view of Sugar Loaf shows the rope tow engine housed in an old bus. Note the line of trees on the left that kept the rope tow separate from the open slope. *Courtesy of Jim Frenette.*

"astonishing" and reported that local skiers were "rapidly improving." On February 9, 1941, an amateur ski meet was held with hundreds in attendance. Shortly afterward, colored lights and floodlights were installed by a crew led by J. Gordon Bisson, allowing night skiing for the last few weeks of the season.

After a successful first season, plans were immediately drawn up to further improve the area. A new rope tow line on the right-hand side of the slope was cleared, and a $500 new Ford V8 engine was secured for the rope tow. The new tow was nearly one thousand feet in length, which took advantage of a steeper pitch at the top of the slope.

With these improvements, Sugar Loaf was poised for an excellent upcoming season. However, when World War II broke out that December, there were greater concerns. A winter carnival was held at Sugar Loaf that season, but soon local men were drafted, and the facility was used less in the following several years. Still, it did manage to operate from time to time during the war years, unlike several other smaller ski areas that closed for good during that period. The 1944–45 season was declared one of the best to date.

With the conclusion of the war, a second growth phase at Sugar Loaf commenced, as returning soldiers increased demand for skiing facilities. For the 1945–46 ski season, the lift was extended even farther up the slope and was now 1,500 feet in length. Sugar Loaf raised money by selling one-dollar membership cards. The money was used for further expansion of ski trails, including an expanded lodge and five miles of additional ski trails surrounding the property. The membership cards allowed skiers to purchase tickets for the bargain rate of fifty cents and helped create a feeling of personal ownership of the ski area.

And with the growth of the area came the ability to host special events. One event was the Intercollegiate Ski Meet, held on March 9, 1947, with colleges and universities throughout the region participating. Organized by Syracuse University Ski Team Coach George F. Earle, the event was a huge success, with great support from the community. He was quoted in a *Tupper Lake Free Press* article as having "never experienced finer hospitality than was extended by Tupper Lake and its Chamber of Commerce, from the moment we arrived right through to the time of departure."

Tragically, just as the ski area was enjoying its height of popularity, a young skier was severely injured while using the rope tow in 1949. A lawsuit filed against Tupper Lake succeeded in court. Despite attempts to open Sugar Loaf for the 1949–50 season, insurance could not be procured, and the facility became dormant. The future did not appear bright for Sugar Loaf.

Many local skiers, dismayed at the closing of the area, worked hard to remedy the situation and reboot the area. These skiers had grown up at Sugar Loaf and wanted to ensure that their children would have a place to ski in town. Members of the Tupper Lake Winter Sports Club, including President Robert Richer, Vice-President Donald Adams, Secretary/Treasurer Juliet Proulx, Bill Frenette, Muriel Ginsburg, Major Day and Fred Baker, worked hard to drum up support for the reopening. In 1955, a $4,895 referendum was drawn up to reopen the ski area and provide full insurance. A meeting held in March 1956 at the Adams Garage helped raise further awareness for the reopening. Dr. Emil Szaaz cited the recent Olympics in Cortina d'Ampezzo, Italy, as proof of the value of skiing and exercise. At the meeting, the strong support from residents passed the referendum.

With the passage, work could begin immediately to restore Sugar Loaf. Over the summer and fall of 1956, the slope was cleared and the rope tow rebuilt, using nineteen poles purchased from Mr. Sykes of Conifer for four dollars each. A caretaker's cabin at the Setting Pole Rapids Dam seven miles away was moved to Sugar Loaf in December 1956 to serve as the new base lodge. William LaValley, superintendent of highways, oversaw the process.

After an eight-year closure, Sugar Loaf reopened for the 1956–57 season. The area quickly regained its popularity and was often packed with skiers, as shown in the 1957 view. *Courtesy of the Goff-Nelson Memorial Library.*

The grand opening was held on January 5, 1957, and Sugar Loaf once again became a thriving ski area. Students were given free transportation to and free skiing at the area, thanks to financial support provided by Tupper Lake. In February, the Oval Wood Dish Invitational Giant Slalom was held, an event that drew hundreds of skiers to the slopes. This event was held in subsequent years as well and became a tradition at Sugar Loaf. Nearly four thousand skier visits were recorded during the winter of 1957, and the first season in years was declared a success.

More improvements took place for the 1957–58 season, with the open slope cleared even higher up on the mountain, new toilet facilities and the return of night skiing. Ticket prices were raised to seventy-five cents a day for adults but remained free for children under eighteen.

In December 1958, volunteer Bill Frenette, who had been associated with Sugar Loaf from the beginning, was quoted in a *Tupper Lake Free Press* article fully supporting the reasoning behind why the ski area was so important.

The quote sums up perfectly the role that small ski areas had and continue to have in the Adirondacks:

> *We've said it before, in this column, and we'll say it again, skiing is a sport indigenous to the North Country. It is also a sport long recognized by physical education authorities not only for its healthful exercise, but for its excellent carry-over value—you can enjoy skiing for example, long after you are unable to play basketball or run track/and in Europe and Canada it is not at all uncommon to see skiers, in their mid-seventies, having a wonderful time and still enjoying life to the fullest.*
>
> *And you'll find universal and loud applause from parents and elders too. What an improvement over being a slave to that white light, or sitting in the movies on a fine Saturday afternoon! What an antidote for standing on the corner with nothing to do, this skiing business!*

The Oval Wood Dish and Tupper Lake Winter Sports Club Giant Slalom was an annual event in the late 1950s. The twelve- to fourteen-year-old class in 1959 was won by William Stevenson. *Courtesy of William Stevenson.*

During the 1958–59 season, which was later declared to be the best ever, business groups and the community began looking at another location for an expanded ski area, as it was becoming clear that no matter how wonderful Sugar Loaf was, its capacity was limited. A much larger mountain, Mount Morris, a very short distance away from Sugar Loaf, was investigated for the site of a new ski area. A proposal for this new development, which would be called Big Tupper, was defeated in 1959, and skiing at Sugar Loaf continued. A fire at the rope tow in February 1960 damaged the lift, and although repairs were made, 1960 would be the final year for skiing at Sugar Loaf.

Plans for Big Tupper were approved in early 1960, and construction began that summer. All of the facilities at Sugar Loaf were moved to Big Tupper—including the rope tow, which would serve its practice slope, lights for night skiing and the ski hut itself, which was turned into a garage. A declaration of thanks to the Oval Wood Dish Company was issued in support of its decades-long donation of land use for Big Tupper. In the spring of 1961, the slope was planted with trees, and the once-active Sugar Loaf Ski Area faded away into history, though its impact continues to be felt decades later. In the memories of lifelong skier Jim Frenette, "If it wasn't for Sugar Loaf, there wouldn't be a Big Tupper."

Visiting the Area

Since Sugar Loaf has been lost for over fifty years, only a few traces of the ski area remain today. The slope has become completely reforested, and there are no remaining cleared areas. There is one rope tow pulley attached to a tree, about fifty yards up the slope, along with portions of the engine at the summit. The former slope can be viewed from a few different vantage points.

As you drive up Ski Tow Road and through the Tupper Lake Golf Club, you will pass the third hole on the right. The ski slope was immediately behind (south) of this hole, and if you look closely, you may be able to distinguish the former ski slope from the surrounding forest. Or, if you are enjoying the golf course, take a look from the third hole up the slope and reflect on its rich history. For more information on the Tupper Lake Golf Club, please visit www.tupperlakegolf.com.

III

Lost Ski Areas of the Whiteface and Keene Valley Regions

The Whiteface and Keene Valley Regions are home to a wide variety of lost ski areas—from the largest vertical-drop ski area to ever permanently close east of the Mississippi River at Whiteface/Marble Mountain to the short and mostly private rope tow that operated at the Quaker Lodge. The area was also home to the largest resort to close in the northern Adirondacks, Paleface.

In the 1930s, a class A racing trail was developed on what is now known as Whiteface Mountain. While used for only a few years, it was one of the most challenging runs in the state. It was not lift-served and required quite a hike to reach the top.

Following this development, two rope tow ski areas opened, in Elizabethtown and in Keene Valley. Both were operated by enthusiastic ski clubs, but only the one in Elizabethtown persisted beyond World War II. It closed in 1959, but a new ski area was developed in the 1960s, using some of the same slopes. The ski area, called Otis Mountain, still operates to this day on a semi-private basis.

At Whiteface/Marble Mountain, New York State built the highest vertical ski area in the state and the highest of its time in the entire Northeast in the 1940s. This complex, consisting of a T-bar, multiple rope tows, a dedicated Sno-Cat transportation system and plentiful trails (designed by Otto Schniebs and Hannes Schneider), had a lot of potential to become one of the East's most popular areas. Unfortunately, high winds often swept the trails clear of snow. It was abandoned in 1960 after a new area, also called Whiteface, was developed on the other side of the ridge. Whiteface, of course, would go on to host the 1980 Winter Olympic alpine events.

Paleface Mountain in Jay was the only true resort in the northern Adirondacks to close. Open from the 1960s into the early 1980s, it featured a chairlift, T-bar, motel, swimming pool, a dude ranch and a restaurant. Ownership changes and poor snowfall resulted in its closure in 1983, and while intact today, it is a private estate and is inaccessible to the public.

ELIZABETHTOWN SKI CENTER

Elizabethtown, New York

1940–1959

The Elizabethtown Ski Center operated for nearly twenty years and was the precursor to the later Otis Mountain development. This area is unique in that it was open, then closed, then reopened as Otis Mountain, then closed and is now open again on a semi-private basis as Otis Mountain. As this was the first phase that was originally abandoned, it will be covered as a lost area.

Founded by the Elizabethtown Ski Club, the center was located about two miles south of town, on the Harry Lobdell Farm. In late 1939, a six-hundred-foot-long rope tow was constructed on a cleared slope, which opened on January 23, 1940, following a recent snowfall. The day was named in honor of Otto Schniebs, the founder of the American Ski School. Schniebs attended the celebration. In February, the first annual ski meet was held; the tradition continued for the next decade.

Following the first season, significant improvements were developed for 1940–41. Cliff and Harry Lobdell, along with club vice-president George Egglefield, spent the summer of 1940 clearing a two-thousand-foot-long open slalom slope, which would be "excelled by none in the North Country." The rope tow was moved from the original slope to the new one and was extended to one thousand feet, providing a larger vertical drop. All of the new improvements brought an air of excitement. Reporter Harry Coonrod of the *Au Sable Forks Record-Post* commented on the benefits of this area and how residents could now look forward to winter in an October 10, 1940 editorial:

> *Thus we of Elizabethtown wait, not regretfully as in some past years for the advent of snow. It is refreshing that so many of both adults and younger sports fans are taking a real interest in this community's participation in winter sports—no village or town throughout this land can help being better, when its citizens find time to play—and enjoy it. The Elizabethtown Ski Club, its officers, its members and its supporters merit the congratulations of the entire community. This reporter joins heartily in its recommendation.*

And indeed, the new slope was used frequently during the second season of operation, including an interscholastic ski meet held on February 1, organized by Wayne Merrick. Fittingly, Elizabethtown won the competition.

While skiing was limited at the area during World War II, the annual ski meet was still held, and the tow continued to operate during weekends into the 1950s. In 1958, improvements were made at the area, with a new nylon rope for the tow and a new children's slope. Ticket prices remained affordable into the late 1950s, at just $1.50 per adult, the equivalent of $12.00 in 2014.

Despite the improvements, the ski area would shut in 1959, likely due to the migration of skiers to developing larger ski areas nearby and a wane in membership of the ski club. The area would remain unused for several years but would be used again in the 1960s as a brand-new ski area—Otis Mountain.

Visiting the Area

For more information on Otis Mountain, please see its section in chapter six.

Paleface/Bassett Mountain

Jay, New York

1961–1981 as Paleface, 1981–1983 as Bassett Mountain

By far the largest privately owned ski area to close in the northern Adirondacks, Paleface was a complete year-round resort with much to offer to skiers and non-skiers alike. Its name was a nod to nearby Whiteface, which was visible from its upper slopes. In addition, most of its trails and features contained Native American references. Although its trails are still maintained by the landowner, it is on private property—under no circumstances try to explore it.

By 1960, the immediate Wilmington-Jay region was without a privately operated ski area. While nearby Whiteface was grand and offered much to the skier, it had lodging and was a state-run venture. Seeing an opportunity to create a complete resort, Reverend Boylan Fitz-Gerald, editor of the *Artist* magazine, and his wife, Jean, purchased six hundred acres that were formerly owned by Dana Peck in early 1960.

Fitz-Gerald announced the $500,000 ski development in April 1960, using private family funds. The original plan for the ski area was to have two moderately long Pomalifts. This idea was quickly abandoned, and a Mueller-brand double chair was ordered instead. This chair would be located close to the base lodge and motel. During late spring and summer, the line for this lift was cleared, and loggers and graders worked quickly to clear the ski trails. Of particular note was that these trails were cleared through an attractive evergreen forest, which also helped shield the trails from sun and wind. The Brave trail was described as the most scenic. Most of the trails were in the beginner to intermediate range and were straight down the fall line. Another expert section, higher up on Bassett Mountain, was located but would not be developed for a few years.

For the base area, a spacious lodge was constructed during the summer and fall of 1960, with a restaurant with plenty of seating, along with three lounges. An adjacent motel for ninety-six guests was also built, providing ski-and-stay benefits that were hard to match at other areas. Skiers would be able to walk just a few hundred feet from their rooms to the ski lift.

Efforts were also made to build a ski school program that would be ready for the following season. Karl and Putzi Jost were hired to operate the ski school. Both were top-notch instructors, with Karl having taught skiing previously at Mount Snow, in Vermont, and Grey Rocks Inn, in Quebec. He was also an accomplished racer.

Walter Prager, another well-known and accomplished skier, was brought in to run the ski shop. This would be his second location, with the other a short distance away in Wilmington. Prager's resume was extensive—from coaching the Dartmouth College Ski Team, to managing Mount Snow, to serving in the Tenth Mountain Division ski troops.

By September 1960, all of the trails that would be open for the first season had been cleared, graded and seeded. An upper mountain shelter, a chalet named the Smoke Rise Lookout, was completed and featured a panoramic view toward Whiteface. The chairlift towers were in place by the end of September, with the lift completed in December.

Although the ski area missed its target opening date in December, all was ready for the grand opening party a month later. On January 21, 1961, over one thousand guests thronged Paleface to officially open the ski area. Many people connected to the ski industry were in attendance, including ski jumper Art Devlin, Whiteface Mountain director Mike Muiry, Walter Prager and the Josts. Kay Eldred smacked a bottle of champagne into the chairlift, and a short time later, Boylan Fitz-Gerald and his daughter Pattie were the first to take the chairlift to the top. Although the skiing was firm, the trails were in good shape, and the first weekend of operation was a success.

In fact, the area so impressed the local community that on February 2, 1961, the *Record-Post* of Au Sable, New York, ran an editorial praising the Fitz-Geralds for building such a magnificent ski area, with its hopes of attracting tourists and skiers from far and wide to come to the area. They also praised the area for hiring locals and decreasing unemployment.

Paleface enjoyed a good rest of the season, as well as the 1961–62 one, when more and more skiers discovered the slopes and slopeside lodging. However, despite how scenic the trails were, they did not offer much to the expert. This was remedied in 1963, with the addition of the Big Horn expert area.

In June 1963, Paleface purchased a new T-bar from Hall Ski Lifts of Watertown, New York. The new lift was over 1,800 feet in length with a vertical of about 500 feet. With a speed of 500 feet per minute, the lift allowed experts to make many runs in rapid succession. Several new trails were cut in this area, including the super-steep Snow Eagle with its 40 percent grade, and the expert Big Horn and Crazy Horse runs. Intermediates could use this lift, too, but would need to exit from the

The Mueller double chair at Paleface was the main ski lift and featured safety bars that swung in from the side, instead of from the top like with modern double chair lifts. Note the freshly groomed snow under the chair. *From a Paleface brochure, courtesy of Woodward Bousquet.*

midstation, where they could enjoy the Teepee, Bow and Peace Pipe trails. Dana Peck, the former landowner, oversaw the installation, which was completed in late October.

The completion of the T-bar area boosted the vertical drop to 730 feet and truly made Paleface "the Adirondacks' Only Complete Ski Resort." No other area could offer all of the facilities that Paleface did. Throughout the rest of the decade, it advertised itself as having "Luxury Holidays at Everyman's Price" and boasted that one could "Park your car and forget it for a whole week!"

Fickle weather and a lack of initial snowmaking did hurt the resort at times, particularly during Christmas 1964, when a thaw and washout ruined skiing across the region. During that holiday, Paleface lost up to $2,000 per day but was better off than other areas, as the resort wasn't entirely dependent on skiing.

To counteract the effects of poor snowfalls, ground crews worked hard to make the trails as smooth as possible to ski on a bare minimum of snowfall. For the 1965–66 season, $50,000 worth of improvements came to Paleface. A Larchmont snowmaking machine was purchased in an effort to guarantee snow. It would cover two trails, the Paleface Trail and the Chairlift Trail. A three-hundred-foot well was drilled to provide adequate water, and over a mile of pipe, with eight hookups, was built along the trails. Other improvements included an indoor pool, which would provide an extra source of recreation if the skiing was limited. The snowmaking machine proved its worth rather quickly, as in January 1966 there was a lack of snowfall—yet Paleface was able to operate on its two snowmaking trails. This allowed the Ausable Valley Jaycees Skate and Ski Spectacular to go on as planned. Night skiing was also added around this time, to provide for more hours of operation.

Opposite, top: This undated, but likely late 1960s, trail map shows the extensive network of downhill runs for all levels of skiers. On the lower left was the chairlift section, with mostly beginner to intermediate fall line trails through evergreen forests. From the top of the chairlift, experts seeking more difficult terrain could take the Squaw Trail to the Big Horn expert section. Intermediates could ride the lift as well, disembarking at the Big Rock Midstation. *Courtesy of the Adirondack Museum.*

Opposite, bottom: The Paleface resort offered a wide selection of summertime activities. The motel and lodge is seen at the top. At the lower left is the dude ranch, and on the right are the summer chairlift rides.

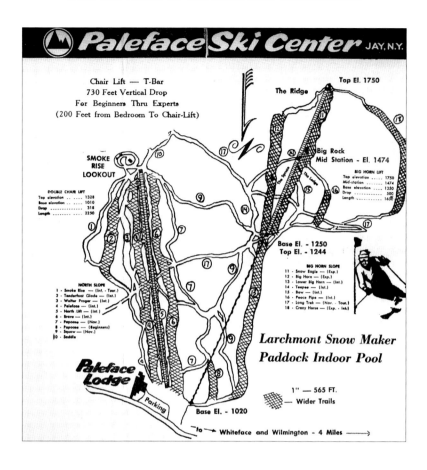

Changes came to the ski school in 1966–67, when Karl Jost left to become a traveling ski instructor certifier, and his wife, Potzi, took over the ski school. Like her husband, she had excellent credentials and had also taught at Mount Snow and Grey Rocks.

Summertime activities were quite popular during the 1960s, when Paleface was transformed into a dude ranch. Guests could ride horses all over the ski trails to enjoy the views. By 1967, over twenty-five horses were at the ranch, and wranglers from Montana were brought in for various shows. The owners advertised the dude ranch as the "best West in the East."

On the eve of the tenth anniversary of Paleface, the owners took out an advertisement in the *Au Sable Record-Post* in November 1969. Here, they thanked the community and their guests for all of their support over the past ten years. They had built a complete resort from scratch, which now offered amenities for all and where the ski area had become "The Family Fun Place, where Everybody knows Everybody!" It was poised for much success as it entered the 1970s.

Unfortunately, Mother Nature had other plans. A string of poor winters from 1971 to 1977 hit the area hard, with less snow than normal, warmer temperatures and rains. It was so bad that, in January 1972, Fitzgerald had to lay off his employees and said that the poor winter had made the area a "disaster area." Another poor year followed for the next season, with only forty-two days in operation. It would have been even fewer if the area had not installed snowmaking.

More snowmaking pipe and snow guns were added in the late 1970s, which helped the area remain in business longer than a lot of other Adirondack areas. By 1979, the Fitz-Geralds had decided to move on and sell the property to Adirondack Concepts Incorporated, a development company. It wished to "rejuvenate" Paleface with the addition of forty condominiums, but this was not approved by the Adirondack Park Agency, which wanted to limit the project to twenty-six. Then, the area was hit by two nearly snowless winters in a row, from 1979 to 1981. By late 1981, in a last ditch effort, the Paleface name was shrugged off and was replaced with Bassett Mountain, the name of the mountain on which the ski area was actually located. Bassett limped along for a couple more seasons but ended up closing in 1983.

Most of the infrastructure remained at the area, including the lodge and lifts, but the snowmaking equipment, no longer needed but still valuable, was sold to Big Tupper in Tupper Lake for $30,000. This included "five fan-jet snow guns and trailers, complete nozzles and assorted amounts of water hose." A 1979 vintage snow groomer was also sold to Big Tupper.

Bassett Mountain was the final incarnation of Paleface and closed in 1983. This promotional brochure featured photos of ski areas from the western United States, perhaps as a marketing move.

The property remained in private hands, and for a while, *Adirondack Life* magazine rented out offices in the base complex. Today, the property is a private estate and cannot be visited by the public for any reason.

Visiting the Area

As previously mentioned, one cannot visit the ski area for any reason. However, one can catch an excellent view of the Big Horn expert area. From the center of Jay, travel west on Route 86 for 1.8 miles. Here, you will pass the entrance for the former resort. Continue driving for another two-thirds of a mile and pull off to the side of the road. Behind you, and across the field, is a view of the expert section. As you can see, the trails here, while short, were extremely steep.

KEENE VALLEY SKI CLUB

Keene Valley, New York

1938–circa 1943

The Keene Valley Ski Club briefly operated in the late 1930s and early 1940s and was part of a winter development in the region. The surrounding region already had several ski trails and even a ski jump. It was located midway between Keene Valley and Keene, on what is now Route 73.

Hal Burton, who had designed a ski trail on Rooster Comb Mountain, along with a gladed ski trail near Marcy Field, initiated the development. He also helped raise money for the Keene Valley Ski Club through the Adirondack Mountain Club, believing that cooperating on terrain would be a "mutually beneficial development," as it would help increase traffic for the Johns Brook Lodge.

With this support, the club opened a 600-foot-long rope tow on an open slope, with a vertical drop of 150 feet. Ray Trumbull, a member of the club, was asked to build and open the tow. He built the tow, and it opened on January 29, 1938. Like many ski clubs, the ski area was only open to members, but membership costs were relatively low, and a membership allowed as much skiing as one could fit in.

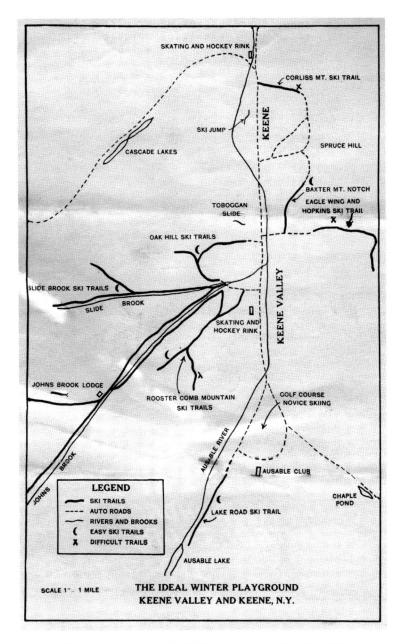

The following text appears within the map image:

SKATING AND HOCKEY RINK

CORLISS MT. SKI TRAIL

KEENE

SKI JUMP

SPRUCE HILL

CASCADE LAKES

BAXTER MT. NOTCH

EAGLE WING AND
HOPKINS SKI TRAIL

TOBOGGAN
SLIDE

OAK HILL SKI TRAILS

KEENE VALLEY

SLIDE BROOK SKI TRAILS

SLIDE   BROOK

SKATING AND
HOCKEY RINK

JOHNS BROOK LODGE

ROOSTER COMB MOUNTAIN
SKI TRAILS

GOLF COURSE
NOVICE SKIING

AUSABLE RIVER

JOHNS   BROOK

AUSABLE CLUB

CHAPLE
POND

LEGEND
——— SKI TRAILS
----- AUTO ROADS
~~~ RIVERS AND BROOKS
(EASY SKI TRAILS
X DIFFICULT TRAILS

LAKE ROAD SKI TRAIL

AUSABLE LAKE

SCALE 1" = 1 MILE

THE IDEAL WINTER PLAYGROUND
KEENE VALLEY AND KEENE, N.Y.

Keene Valley was described in this 1938 map as being "The Ideal Winter Playground." Nearby ski trails were located on Corliss Mountain and Roster Comb Mountain. A ski jump was located closer to Keene, along with a toboggan slide. The location of the ski tow was not marked. *From the January 1938 Adirondack Mountain Club Bulletin, courtesy of the New England Ski Museum.*

By the 1941–42 season, membership had grown to sixty-eight, and improvements were made to the tow, with the engine moved to the summit for better efficiency. To help expand membership and raise funds, the club held several fundraisers during this time, including sleigh rides and pancake breakfasts.

As World War II progressed, the ski club folded, and skiing came to an end at the tow. It is not known what became of the lift.

Visiting the Area

The location of the rope tow did not appear on any maps, so the exact location is unknown. However, it was described as being halfway between Keene and Keene Valley, which would put it near Marcy Field. Having been closed for over seventy years, there are likely no remnants.

QUAKER MOUNTAIN LODGE

Wilmington, New York

1948–1956

The Quaker Mountain Lodge ski area in Wilmington was a semi-private ski area, used mostly for guests, as well as neighbors and friends. It was a rope tow ski area with a single, short slope that was ideal for beginners and newcomers to the sport. Most of this account of its history is thanks to an oral interview with Sidney Maxwell, by Karen Peters of the Wilmington Historical Society.

Like so many ski areas in the region, this one has ties to Otto Schniebs, as he originally owned the lodge. In 1945, Schniebs had heard rumors that someone was going to purchase the property across the street and open a "whoopee house," according to Maxwell. He convinced his friends Johnny and Sidney Maxwell, who were looking to buy a camp, to purchase the area prior to the other interested party doing so. The Maxwells then built a camp on the property.

In 1948, Otto Schniebs and his wife, Frida, decided to sell the lodge and move closer to Wilmington. At the time, the lodge was surrounded by thick

Although it is hard to see in this undated photo of the Quaker Mountain Lodge, the ski slope can just barely be made out behind it. This view is looking east on Quaker Mountain Road.

forests. It had a limited view and was quite dark, and Frida had wanted one with more light. Later on, when the area was cleared for the ski slope and the lodge renovated, Frida commented that they never should have sold the place.

The new owner of the lodge was John J. "Donna" Fox, an accomplished bobsledder and former captain of the American team. He immediately went about renovating the lodge, adding bedrooms, along with a bar in the basement called the Fox Den, which Maxwell remembers as being quite popular.

Wishing to build a ski area, Fox hired Mr. Olney to clear a line of trees (using handsaws) in the back of the lodge leading to Quaker Mountain Road. A rope tow was installed on the right-hand side of the slope facing downhill, and the area opened for the 1948–49 season. It was geared mainly toward guests, who were often famous, including Jackie Gleason and Dick Button, who enjoyed its seclusion.

The Maxwells were allowed to use the area, thanks to the kindness of Fox. Oftentimes their friends would join them on the slope after a day of skiing at Marble Mountain. They would return home after skiing there, enjoy "a cheery drink" and then proceed to ski at Quaker Mountain Lodge. They often used the area to teach many of their friends and family who were visiting how to ski.

In addition, they often enjoyed the area with their sons, Tom and Jack, who were young at the time. They let the children ski down the slope and then wait for them at the bottom, as riding the tow by themselves was too difficult—or so they thought. Sidney Maxwell noted that "we looked down the tow, and here is Jack who was three years old at the time coming up the tow all by himself, with a big grin on his face, so proud that he had grabbed onto that tow all by himself."

Tragically, in April 1956, Donna Fox passed away, and according to Maxwell, this ended the skiing at the lodge.

Visiting the Area

Quaker Mountain Lodge is a private home and thus cannot be visited. The ski area portion of the property is now mostly wooded. Reportedly, the engine for the tow is still visible in the forest.

Santa's Workshop

Wilmington, New York

Circa 1950

One of the more mysterious lost areas in the northern Adirondacks was a rope tow at Santa's Workshop in Wilmington. In 1950, a *Ski New York Guidebook* listed the area in the following manner:

> *Santa's Workshop, at Whiteface Mountain, has a ski tow for children. It is one mile from the Whiteface Ski Center and parents who want to ski the Whiteface trails will find Santa's tow a convenient place to park the children. Admission is $0.76 for adults, free to children under ten.*

Despite such a specific listing, no other contemporary literature ever mentioned this ski area, and it is quite possible that it never existed. If it did, it was most certainly brief and, as the advertisement stated, would have been used as an alternative area for young children from nearby Whiteface.

Visiting the Area

The exact location of the rope tow at Santa's Workshop is unknown, as is whether it even existed. However, Santa's Workshop itself is in full operation, with more information available at www.northpoleny.com.

Whiteface Mountain Ski Center/ Marble Mountain

Wilmington, New York

1949–1960

The original Whiteface Mountain Ski Center, also referred to as Marble Mountain was the boldest and largest ski area development ever to close in the state and has the record for the largest vertical drop ski area to close east of the Mississippi. On paper, it looked like the area would have been incredibly successful, with six ski lifts, including a T-bar; numerous trails; a handsome base lodge; and an eye-popping 2,500-foot vertical drop. Instead, it had a fatal flaw that prevented it from becoming a true success. It was replaced by the nearby Whiteface Mountain development that continues to thrive today.

In the late 1930s, several northeastern United States ski areas with significant vertical drops were being developed, including Mount Mansfield in Stowe, Vermont, and Cannon Mountain in Franconia, New Hampshire. New York State did not have any ski areas with substantial verticals during that time, and local residents and business owners wanted to remedy this situation.

On February 15, 1940, the Whiteface Area Ski Council was formed in North Elba, consisting of representatives from local towns, ski clubs and businesses. The Adirondack Mountain Club recommended that Whiteface Mountain, with its sustained pitches and recently built Whiteface Mountain Highway, would make a perfect spot for a ski area to develop. In addition, it was far enough away from the High Peaks region so as to not adversely affect that wilderness region. Another meeting was held in November to further plans and featured Otto Schniebs as a speaker.

In order to develop the ski area, a New York State constitutional amendment would need to pass to authorize its construction. This did not take much convincing, as New York State was doing all it could to continue to minimize the state of the Depression. In the senate, the bill was sponsored by Benjamin Feinberg, and in the assembly by Sheldon Weeks, and it was named Amendment Four. It went to voters and passed in the November election.

But World War II broke out just after the passage of the amendment and stymied any development plans. Immediately following the war, the newly created Whiteface Mountain Authority immediately made firmer plans to develop the ski area. In October 1945, survey teams scoured the Whiteface Mountain area, looking for a location to build the lifts. Initially, a nine-thousand-foot-long chairlift was proposed on the east side of Whiteface (near the location of the present ski area), along with a T-bar lift down Marble Mountain. It was expected that with this surveying, the ski area could be developed and open in time for the 1946–47 season, but that would not occur for several more years. However, one ski trail on the Marble Mountain side was partially cleared and graded in 1945.

In August 1946, the plans were modified again, with the nine-thousand-foot-long lift broken up into two separate lifts. Plans also called for the exclusion of rope tows; instead, "the skier will revel in the luxury of being transported skyward by a 2,700-foot T-bar lift" on the Marble Mountain side. These plans would change, too, with the chairlift concept abandoned and several locations for rope tows added for Marble Mountain. A cost estimate of $350,000 was determined for the first phase of the development, with the eventual goal of developing the Whiteface Mountain side.

More delays cropped up in 1946. The cost of getting workers to the site was extensive, as there was no road yet to the bottom of the T-bar because New York State did not own the land for the road. Even with this delay, three out of the four major ski trails were finished by 1946, and a road to the bottom of the T-bar would be built by 1948, once land was obtained from private owners. The ski trails were laid out by two of skiing's finest masters—Otto Schniebs and Hannes Schneider. Schneider was a famous Austrian instructor who developed the Arlberg technique and operated a thriving ski school at Cranmore Mountain, New Hampshire, among other accomplishments.

Overseeing the development was manager Arthur Draper, a former member of the Tenth Mountain Division. He hired forty Seabees to work on the clearing of the ski trails.

The lower section of trail number one, the Lowell Thomas Trail, led skiers back to the base of the T-bar. The trail was quite steep and was often used for downhill races.

In October and November 1947, clearing of the $128,000 Roebling T-bar lift line began. This lift would have a vertical drop of nine hundred feet and would be the most substantial lift in the Adirondacks. It would be over three thousand feet in length and carry seven hundred skiers per hour. It, too, would be delayed, due to a lack of steel for the lift towers. While the area could have opened with a rope tow, Draper decided against this because it would have been a rather modest opening.

The T-bar at Marble Mountain was the longest ski lift in the Adirondacks until the modern Whiteface was developed. The lift provided an easy ascent as compared to riding rope tows. Today, this lift line is a hiking trail with all of the lift foundations still present.

The Roebling T-bar was located below the base lodge. This skier is looking up the lift line, which gave skiers several interesting, twisting trails. If you look closely behind the T-bar, you can make out the trail that took skiers to the Ski School Slope.

The practice slope featured a rope tow, and this slope, which had a 10 percent grade, was perfect for beginners. Scattered trees were left standing to make the slope more interesting. The tow was located on the skiers' left, just out of view in this picture.

By October 1948, the T-bar was finally completed. It was operational in December to transport materials to the top of the ski area, using temporary chairs attached to the cable. Workers enjoyed a ride back down the lift at the end of the workday.

Also finished during this time was a spectacular $200,000 base lodge. Inside was a full cafeteria and large sitting areas, a wax room, first aid station and communication station. It featured a panoramic view of the slopes. By Christmas, the ski area was ready to welcome its first skiers.

What they found was an impressive facility—and here is how all of the sections of the ski area fit together. Upon arrival at the lodge, skiers had several options. They could use a practice slope with a rope tow below the parking lot or ski down a trail to the bottom of the T-bar. If they wished to return to the lodge, they could take a free, short and steep rope tow from near the base of the T-bar. From the bottom of the T-bar was another trail that connected to the Ski School Slope and rope tow.

If they choose to ride the T-bar, four trails and a slalom slope were available. Looking up the T-bar, the slalom slope was on the far left, followed by the 5,000-foot-long Lowell Thomas Trail , the 3,500-foot-long Harry Wade Hicks Trail, the 3,500-foot-long Hubert Stevens Trail and the 7,500-foot-long Otto Schniebs Trail. Also available were Sno-Cat rides on a trailer up the Whiteface Memorial Highway to the Sno-Cat Trail, which led up to another skiing area at the 4,400-foot level. Skiers could be taken up in groups of thirty to enjoy the high elevation, narrow trails and two rope tows that served them. Once done, they would ski down the Wilmington Trail back to the top of the T-bar, a total vertical of 2,500 feet, impressive even by today's standard. If they wished, they could also stop at the Lookout Mountain Shelter at the top, which featured a snack bar. Scattered about the mountain were twelve first aid caches, which stored supplies and toboggans, with a certified ski patrol to assist in the case of an accident. Even lodging was available in two "barracks" (former CCC bunkhouses) that could sleep one hundred near the lodge.

Christmas Day 1948 saw the first skiers in the upper area using the Sno-Cat, with the practice and ski school slopes and tows opening on January 1, 1949. The T-bar would operate for skiers for the first time on January 2. An official grand opening would not be held until February 19, with Governor Thomas E. Dewey in attendance.

It was during the first few seasons that Marble Mountain's fatal flaw was discovered: howling, persistent wind. Although snowfall was relatively plentiful, it was quickly blown away or turned into ice by these winds. This severely limited operation of the T-bar trails, and a good part of the time

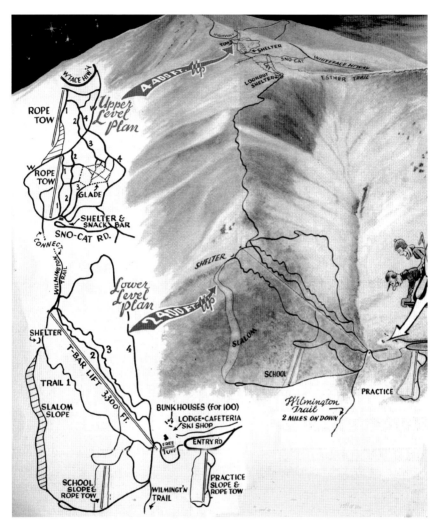

A circa 1950 brochure for the Whiteface Ski Center shows the extensive facilities available for skiers. Note the practice slope below the entry road, the T-bar and the four trails/slalom slope it served, the distant Ski School Slope and rope tow and the upper-level section with its two tows, trails and glades.

only the beginner tow was in operation. Perhaps with today's modern snowmaking and grooming, the effects of the winds could have been counteracted but didn't exist until well after its closure.

After those first few limited seasons, another streak of bad luck hit Whiteface hard. Its beautiful base lodge, worth $200,000, was destroyed in

Sno-Cats helped transport skiers to the upper section, which was served by two rope tows and featured an interesting mix of trails and glades. Sid Maxwell remembers that the skiing was quite enjoyable but also very cold, the top being the highest lift-served skiing in the northeastern United States.

From the base lodge at Marble Mountain, skiers and non-skiers alike enjoyed a panoramic view of the slopes. From left to right is the Lowell Thomas Trail (trail one), T-bar, Harry Wade Hicks Trail (trail two) and Hubert Stevens Trail (trail three). Out of sight to the right is the Otto Schniebs Trail (trail four).

a blaze on May 6, 1951, that began at 9:00 p.m. Only a few items were salvaged, including some kitchen equipment and a boiler. The cause of the fire was never determined, and the remnants smoldered for weeks.

Backed up by the state, a new lodge was immediately ordered and designed, this one to be made of spruce logs. It was built on the exact footprint of the previous lodge and was partially completed for the 1951–52 season; it was completely finished for the following one.

Adding to the improvements for the 1951–52 season was a new ski school slope, built above the garage and designed by Ron MacKenzie of Lake Placid. The rope tow from the old Ski School Slope was moved to this new location, and its trails, along with the slalom slope, were abandoned as there was no way to return back to base area from the bottom. The isolated location of the Ski School Slope, far away from the base lodge, was the main factor in its closure.

Despite these improvements and upgrades, it was becoming clear that the ski area was not living up to its potential as a major resort designed to attract skiers from far and wide. Local chambers of commerce and business owners asked the state to consider adding chairs to the T-bar or converting it into a chairlift to allow for summertime tourists. Additionally, the area faced a deficit of over $20,000 a year, with no sign of it breaking even anytime soon.

During the few brief times that the weather cooperated, the ski area was thronged with visitors. On February 22, 1954, over three thousand enjoyed the slopes, jamming the parking lot and trails. Area inns and hotels were packed. These days were far and few between, and residents started demanding answers for why this area was failing.

In one editorial in the *Adirondack Daily Enterprise* on September 25, 1956, Sidney T. Cox stated in a scathing review:

> *New York's first attempt to provide large-scale recreation skiing facilities has proven a failure so egregious as to damage the reputation of the entire state as a Winter tourist area…in the two most recent Winters, when New England and other New York ski areas were enjoying their best seasons in history, the Whiteface Mountain Authority's development—an $850,000 investment originally—lost $27,269 and $28,258 respectively.*
>
> *The reason for this fiasco is simple enough: Not enough snow…the record of the number of days of operation of the Whiteface Mountain Ski Center shows clearly that there was not sufficient snow in any year to attract the number of visitors needed to make the project self-*

Skiers are about to disembark the T-bar near the summit. Note the lift attendant's hut on the right. Today, the lift line is much narrower, but easy to follow.

sustaining…The dismal record is therefore all the more noticeable and has made the Adirondack region something of a laughing-stock both in New York and in neighboring states.

The writing was clearly on the wall for the ski area. In 1957, efforts in the state legislature were made to consider other alternatives. The original location for the chairlifts on the east slope was given another look and, in May 1957, the Whiteface Mountain Authority was reorganized to develop this project. Arthur Draper was kept on as a full-time manager. With full state backing, two long chairlifts were ordered, and brand-new trails were cleared. The "new" Whiteface would open in January 1958 and was a dramatic improvement in term of facilities and trails, with less wind. It would go on, of course, to host the Winter Olympics in 1980.

Even with the new development, Marble Mountain operated on weekends and holidays as an overflow area. The snack bar remained operational in the lodge, but that was about it—very little effort was put into keeping the ski area functional. It closed for good at the end of the 1959–60 ski season.

At least two of its lifts went on to be reused at other ski areas. The T-bar sat abandoned for five years, until October 1965, when West Mountain in Queensbury, New York, purchased the lift. It was dismantled later that month and heavily modified into a single chairlift. One tower still stands in the woods on the skiers' right of the Whiteface double chair. A rope tow was sold to Blue Boar, at Camp Pok-O-Moonshine, where it served a beginner slope and toboggan hill.

The Whiteface base lodge still stands proudly today. In 1961, it became the headquarters for the Atmospheric Sciences Research Center, run by the State University of New York at Albany. According to its website, it "includes extensive laboratory and instrument space, offices and a lecture hall." Inside, the original stone fireplace remains, with a large trail map of the ski area. It is generally not open to the public.

Visiting the Area

The former ski area at Marble Mountain presents an excellent opportunity for exploration. The area is accessible by driving on Route 481 west from Wilmington and turning left onto Marble Mountain Lane. At the end of the lane, turn left as the road veers away from the Atmospheric Science Research Center and park on the left. The former practice slope is below the parking lot but is now forest, with nothing to see. From the parking area, look for the trail descending from the road, follow this for a short distance until it merges into a wider dirt road and bear left. After another one-tenth of a mile, you will reach the base of the former T-bar.

Equipment has been installed on the foundation of the T-bar, but it is clearly visible. The lift line is directly ahead of the foundation but is unmarked. The lift line is a 3,300-foot-long hike, 900 feet vertically up the mountain. Along the line, you will see plenty of foundations for the lift towers, as well as a toboggan shelter/cache approximately one-third of the way up. The trail does contain numerous small and loose rocks, so sturdy footwear is recommended. While hiking, look to the right, as remnants of ski trails can just be made out through the forest. The former Ski School Slope is located about one-quarter of a mile east from the lower T-bar but is completely overgrown.

One of the most surprising remnants of Marble Mountain is this toboggan cache located about one-third of the way up the T-bar. It is remarkably intact considering it is over sixty years old. Its heavy-duty construction and elevation above the wet ground likely helped preserve it.

Once you reach the top of the lift line, a large counterweight to the T-bar is on the left, along with expansive views. If you turn right at the end of the line, the trail shortly intersects with the Wilmington Trail, follow signs to hike to the summit of Esther and Whiteface Mountains. There is not a lot to see in this section regarding the former area, as much of the upper section has become overgrown.

No ski trails are clear enough for downhill skiing today, but one could climb up and ski down the lift line, once the deep snows of winter arrive.

IV

Lost Ski Areas of the
Northern Tier and
Saint Lawrence Regions

The Northern Tier and Saint Lawrence regions of northern New York were home to a wide variety of ski areas, from community areas like the Clifton-Fine Lions Club, to university areas like the St. Lawrence Snow Bowl, to resorts with so much potential that was never realized, like at Lowenberg.

The first ski area to develop was a brief rope tow in Canton, at Bullis Woods. Used mostly by St. Lawrence University students, the area was left behind once the Snow Bowl was developed. This new area, complete with major ski jumps, would operate for nearly forty years and was one of the most successful university-owned ski areas in the country. Another smaller, but similar area operated at Clarkson College in the 1950s, which was later followed up by another ski area it would purchase, Seven Springs.

Several ski clubs operated their own areas, too, including at Ellenburg and Black Lake. While small in scale, these areas were excellent training grounds for new skiers and children. Other community rope tow areas, such as Skyline or Polar Valley, were used mainly by local skiers seeking an opportunity to make some runs during the weekend.

One of the more complete ski areas in the northern Adirondacks existed at Juniper Hills. Here, a modern ski lodge sat atop the area, a rarity for most ski areas. Two surface lifts provided for a variety of terrain, with night skiing available. It would close due to poor snowfall in 1980.

The Adirondacks' largest ski area was nearly developed at Lowenberg. Although it was poised to become a massive operation, only a T-bar and a few trails were ever built. Financial difficulties resulted in the area closing, just a few years after it made its debut. Today, its T-bar is nearly intact, rusting away on the hillside, a relic and reminder of what could have been.

Black Lake Ski Center

Black Lake, New York

1949–1950 and 1960–1967

A small but family-friendly ski area once operated on the shores of Black Lake, on the property of Ace and Ann's Lakeside Hotel. It began as a brief rope tow operation for the 1949–50 season and then reopened for much of the 1960s. It featured a wide-open, gentle slope with a limited vertical drop and sweeping views of the lake.

The first phase of the ski area was a rope tow that operated for just one season, in 1949–50. This was owned and operated by Asa Ames at the hotel. When a barn on the property burned, it spread to the rope tow, destroying the lift. The open slope remained devoid of a ski lift throughout the rest of the 1950s; however, local children would occasionally use the slope for sledding and non-lift-served skiing.

In January 1959, Ames was once again enamored with the idea of reopening his ski hill and hosted a meeting on January 29 at the hotel for interested skiers. At the meeting, a new ski club was formed—the Black Lake Ski Club. Harry "Skip" Dailey of Ogdensburg was elected president. Dues were set at just two dollars per year for individual members and four dollars per year for an entire family. Ames also generously agreed to donate the use of his property and allowed the club to use the hotel as headquarters. The area was to be marketed to residents of Canton, Gouverneur, Hammond, Heuvelton, Lisbon and Madrid.

A month later, at a club meeting, the name was changed to the Northern Tier Ski Club, in order to reflect the geographic diversity of its members. The ski area itself would often be referred to as the Black Lake Ski Center though, to clearly identify its location.

By April 1959, membership had grown to thirty-three families, with the eventual goal of reaching one hundred. In October, the number had grown to sixty. Also in October, a new election was held for officers, with Claire

Burns of Ogdensburg becoming the new president. She oversaw the growth of the club, and by winter, over two hundred had become members.

During the fall of 1959, club members worked hard to build facilities for the ski area. Only minimal grading and clearing of the slope was required. A used one-thousand-foot-long ski tow was donated by the St. Lawrence University Snow Bowl, likely one that had been briefly in use near its sixty-meter jump. Members dug the holes for the rope tow poles and cleared rocks from the site.

The tow construction ground to a halt in early 1960, as there was trouble in securing the right type of pulleys for the tow. Even with the delay in opening the lift, the ski area saw much use in January and February 1960. Coach "Doc" Littlejohn from St. Lawrence University came in to teach lessons on several weekends, and many club members used the slope for tobogganing or making runs. The tow was finally completed in March and operated for a few weeks before the snow melted away.

The club made immediate plans for improvements for the following season. Over the summer of 1960, the rope tow was moved to the center of the slope in order to create two distinct runs on each side of the tow, and the rope itself was replaced. John Wilson expertly did the work, at a cost of $1,900. A new metal shed was ordered from Montgomery Ward to house the rope tow motor. Lights for night skiing were installed. Also, a designated toboggan run on the western side of the slope was marked off to prevent skiers from running into sledders. Finally, a small warming hut was erected at the foot of the slope.

The ski club heavily promoted these changes, and by the end of 1960, over three hundred were now members of the club, mostly families from the surrounding area. For the 1960–61 season, Coach "Doc" Littlejohn taught classes and helped establish a basic ski patrol. Unfortunately, there was a lack of snowfall during that second season, which limited the use of the hill.

Over the next few years, the ski area had better seasons, with more consistent snowfall, and the club continued to grow. The area marketed itself to St. Lawrence University students as an alternative to its Snow Bowl area, advertising the benefit of having a ski area close to the hotel, where students could enjoy food and music after their day on the slopes.

In 1964, the ski center, along with other nearby areas, jointly advertised, calling themselves the North Star Slopes. The Black Lake area was described in the following manner in this advertisement:

Skiing in the old tradition is wintertime fun at BLACK LAKE. Tiny tots may romp, roll downhill and ski and slide to their heart's content. Mothers and dads also thoroughly enjoy themselves on the hill. A rope tow makes it all fun. Just good old-fashioned fun for the entire family, the BLACK LAKE hill is on a splendid country road along the northwest shore of the lake.

The ski area continued to operate until 1967, when membership began to dwindle, and the cost of insurance for the area increased. In addition, there was increasing competition from other nearby areas that offered much larger facilities than the simple slopes at Black Lake. Attempts to raise sufficient cash to open the area for the 1967–68 season were unsuccessful, resulting in the closure of the Black Lake Ski Center.

Visiting the Area

The Black Lake Ski Center was located near the junction of Demot Road and Black Lake Road. A visit by Adam Terko in 2014 confirmed that there are no remnants of this area, and it is on private property, where no trespassing is allowed.

BULLIS WOODS

Canton, New York

1941–circa 1943

Bullis Woods, in Canton, was the location of the first ski area operated by St. Lawrence University. The area, owned by J. Leslie Craig, had been used by skiers in the late 1930s but was not lift-served. Wishing to have a ski area fairly close to campus, the university requested and was granted permission by Craig to build a rope tow and trails, along with a small ski jump. In a 1941 article in the *Canton Commercial-Advertiser*, the area was expected to become a "skier's paradise." A tow was built in late 1941 and would operate for several years.

In early 1942, a Swedish ski export, Inga Grauers, who had been trained by the Hannes Schneider Ski School in Austria, arrived at St. Lawrence to give workshops to the Women's Ski Team. With World War II in full swing, she was unable to return home and stayed for the rest of the season, giving lessons.

The area closed around 1943, likely due to the ongoing war and the soon-to-come development of the St. Lawrence University Snow Bowl, a much larger development.

Visiting the Area

There is nothing left of the former ski area at Bullis Woods, as the State University of New York at Canton, and roads associated with it, were built on the site.

LOWENBERG

Dannemora, New York

1966–1969

Had it been fully developed, Lowenberg Ski Area (German for Lyon Mountain, on which it is located) could have been one of the largest ski areas in the East. Grand plans for this area included up to thirty chairlifts, a vertical drop of over two thousand feet, fifty ski trails, numerous chalets, a European-style village and a marina. At the ski area, only a short T-bar, base lodge and a few trails were ever constructed and operated during its four seasons. Financial problems related to the development led to its closing, and forty-five years later, many remnants of this ski area still exist.

Located a short twenty-two miles from Plattsburgh, and within a reasonable drive from Montreal, Lyon Mountain dominates the surrounding landscape. The mountain is in a favorable location to enhance local snowfalls, and its geography is well-suited for a ski area.

The Lowenberg development was the brainchild of real estate developer Bennett T. Clute from Plattsburgh, who founded the Lowenberg Corporation. Seeing the decline of mining and lumbering in the region, he sought to construct a large-scale recreational facility that would attract tourists and provide local employment. Nine thousand acres of land were either purchased or leased from the Republic Steel Corporation and the Howard Smith Paper Mills Corporation, which had timber rights on Lyon Mountain.

In May 1964, the first advertisement for Lowenberg was posted in the *North Countryman*, setting out the bold goals of the development:

> *Now the name Lowenberg means practically nothing to area residents, but indeed in the near future it will spell an economic upturn the likes of which will brighten the hearts of area businessmen. The problems that have beset our area can be solved by the inducement offered to new industry, but this is a tough uphill battle.*
>
> *The obvious answer to Clinton County's economy, is to take the obvious step of increasing our recreational activities. "LOWENBERG" or as you have known it for years, "Lyon Mountain," will become within the next few years one of the largest skiing developments to be found anywhere east of the Mississippi. The mountain is a good one, it's big, has a very high average snowfall, and its terrain is perfectly suited to a variety of ski runs that will tickle the hearts of the most avid skier.*

The Hall Ski-Lift Company of Watertown, New York, began engineering work for the ski lifts in 1964. A 6,400-foot-long double chairlift to below the summit was to be the first chair installed, along with a 4,000-foot-long T-bar lift to a peak that was to be called "Little Kitz," presumably after the Kitzbuhel resort in Austria. Neither of the lifts was ever actually constructed, however.

As plans for the development continued, Otto Schniebs, the former St. Lawrence University ski coach and the founder of the American Ski School, was brought in as a consultant. In May 1965, he was quoted in the *Plattsburgh Press-Republican* as saying:

> *The various long bowls on the mountain's north and east sides are exceptionally good for all types of skiers. My survey shows that Lowenberg has the potential to be a major and outstanding development in both winter and summer.*

By the late spring of 1965, the road to the base area was built, and a 1,300-foot-long Hall T-bar was built on a ridge just east of what would become the parking lot and base lodge. Several trails and slopes were cleared alongside the 250-foot vertical drop lift, supervised by ski school director Karl Jost. While it appeared that the ski area would open for the 1965–66 ski season, a car accident involving Jost resulted in severe injuries, and as a critical member in the future operation, Clute made the decision to postpone the grand opening

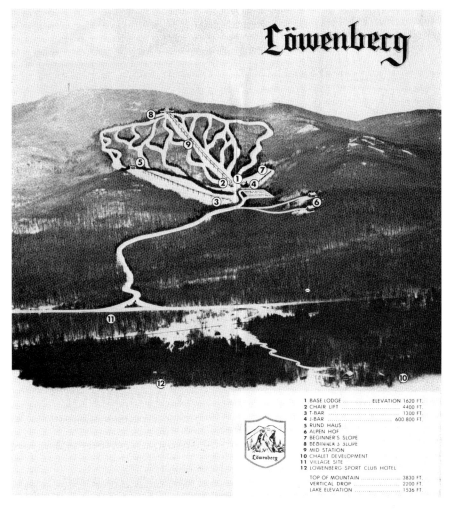

Löwenberg

1 BASE LODGE .... ELEVATION 1620 FT.
2 CHAIR LIFT .... 4400 FT.
3 T-BAR .... 1300 FT.
4 J-BAR .... 600-800 FT.
5 RUND HAUS
6 ALPEN HOF
7 BEGINNER'S SLOPE
8 BEGINNER'S SLOPE
9 MID STATION
10 CHALET DEVELOPMENT
11 VILLAGE SITE
12 LOWENBERG SPORT CLUB HOTEL

TOP OF MOUNTAIN .... 3830 FT.
VERTICAL DROP .... 2200 FT.
LAKE ELEVATION .... 1536 FT.

The initial plan for Lowenberg was grand in scope, including a chairlift, T-bar, J-bar and a dozen trails to start. Only a short T-bar serving four trails, the base lodge and parking lot were ever constructed at the ski area. *Courtesy of the New England Ski Museum.*

another year. Despite this, some skiers took advantage of the recently cleared slopes during early 1966, accessing them by snowmobile.

In the summer of 1966, a forty- by fifty-foot base lodge was partially completed. For the following ski season, it would offer basic shelter and a snack bar. In addition, the Lowenberg Lodge, with a capacity for forty, on the shores of Chazy Lake, was constructed. Paul Bower was hired as general manager, and Robert MacDonald was hired as a maintenance supervisor.

After the closure of Lowenberg, the open slopes were still used for several years by backcountry and cross-country skiers. Here, two skiers enjoy the view from one of the former ski trails toward Chazy Lake in the early 1970s. *Courtesy of Andrew Sajor.*

Due to his injuries and his other job as the chief examiner for the Canadian Ski Instructors Alliance, Jost would be available only part time. In his place, Herman Schmidt was hired as ski school director. The ski patrol would be led by Tom Condon.

Lowenberg managed to open during the last week of December 1966, with four trails in operation. The news spread fast about this new area, gradually growing in popularity, with some weekends hosting one hundred skiers on its limited terrain.

More plans for more chairlifts and a J-bar, an expanded vertical drop and additional trails were announced for the 1967–68 season, but only some upper trails were cleared. And while the area was also enjoyed for the 1968–69 season, the area would shutter by the end of March. It is believed that financial problems combined with the over ambitious plans to result in Lowenberg closing for good in March 1969. By 1973, the area was completely abandoned and the base lodge described as "ramshackle"; it was torn down a few years later. The open ski slopes were still in use for intrepid backcountry and cross-country skiers until the late 1970s, when they became too overgrown and faded back into the Adirondack forest. The T-bar lift remained in place, gradually rusting away, and forty years later it remains one of the most intact former ski lifts in the Northeast.

Visiting the Area

Lowenberg is one of the more accessible and intriguing lost ski areas to discover. Numerous remnants of the ski area remain, including the foundation for the base lodge, a nearly intact T-bar lift and overgrown ski trails. In fact, the T-bar is one of the longest abandoned ski lifts in the Northeast that is still standing. The best time of the year to visit is April through mid-May and again in late October through November, when the trees are bare of leaves.

From the junction of Route 374 and Chazy Lake Road, take Chazy Lake Road south for approximate one and three-quarters miles and turn right onto the dirt Lowenberg Road (sometimes shown on maps as Ski Area Road). Note that this road is not maintained during the winter season. Follow the road for nine-tenths of a mile until the end, where you will find a public parking lot that used to serve the ski area. You can also enjoy a new hiking trail to the summit of 3,820-foot-tall Lyon Mountain from the parking lot.

Looking just to the west of the parking lot, you can make out the foundation of the former ski lodge. The cement slab is slowly being overrun by vegetation.

A few old powerlines are also visible through the woods to the north.

The T-bar was located to the south of the parking lot, across the road and down two hundred feet. The T-bar is nearly intact, minus its motor. The base framework of the T-bar is rusting away and is surrounded by trees but still stands. One can easily follow the T-bar on an

The rusting bottom drive for the T-bar remains standing in the woods to the east of the parking lot forty-five years after last operating. *Courtesy of Kevin Papenfuss.*

The Lowenberg T-bar is nearly intact despite decades of abandonment. Here, one of the towers stands, surrounded by trees. Note the cable still attached. Most of the T's remain attached, particularly higher up the lift line.

approximate fifteen-minute hike to the top. On the way up, notice the rusted towers. In places, the cable has become detached from the towers and is now hanging dozens of feet in the air. The T's themselves still dangle high above the ground, never to be used again.

At the top, the T-bar return station is mostly intact, but corrosion is occurring in the foundations, which may lead to a failure of the structure in the next few decades. Cement foundations can easily be found for the former lift attendant's shack near the unloading area of the ski lift.

The ski trails from the top of the T-bar are quite overgrown and are hard to follow, particularly in the summer. It is easy to become lost, and there is little to see. After exploring the summit, it is recommended to return via the T-bar lift.

However, one of the ski trails can be explored. If you plan to hike to the summit of Lyon Mountain on the new hiking trail from the parking lot, you will initially follow a cut-but-never-opened trail, which was to be used in the second phase of expansion.

Ellenberg Outing Club

Ellenberg, New York

1950–circa 1952

In January 1950, the Ellenberg Outing Club opened a six-hundred-foot-long rope tow on the hillside owned by Norman Sequin. Open slopes of six hundred feet to one thousand feet in length were available, but snowfall was not plentiful that first season, and the skiing was quite limited.

In 1951 and 1952, improvements came to the hill, including a lighted shelter, snack bar and lights for night skiing. Skiing was available mostly on afternoons and on Monday and Wednesday nights, for the very affordable price of fifty cents for adults and twenty-five cents for children.

Despite the affordable prices, it appears that the ski area did not operate much past 1952, ceasing to be listed in guidebooks and newspaper accounts. The exact reason for closure is unknown.

Visiting the Area

As it has been sixty years since the closure, there are no true remnants of this ski area, which is on private property one mile south of Ellenberg on the Plank Road.

Juniper Hills

Harrisville, New York

1964–1980

A family-oriented ski area, Juniper Hills operated for over fifteen years in Harrisville. Advertising itself as "The Biggest Little Hill in the North Country," it had more features than many similar small ski areas, including two overhead cable lifts and a modern base lodge. Although it had a vertical drop of only 170 feet over seventy-two acres, it did offer a good amount of variety of terrain for all levels of skiers.

During the Christmas season of 1963, Jules LaPrairie had the concept of developing a ski area in Harrisville, and this led to the formation of a corporation to make it happen. Working with Verne Wicks, in March 1964, Juniper Hills, Inc. was founded in order to develop a ski area in Harrisville off Route 3, with Wicks as president. The ski area was to be built on property owned by his brother and would feature views of Lake Bonaparte. The State Department of Commerce helped encourage this development, hoping that it would serve as a feeder area for larger ski areas.

Stock was sold at a cost of $100 per share to raise funds for the area's construction. A groundbreaking was held on May 24. During the summer of 1964, trails were blasted and cleared, and a new road was built to the top of the ski area. A rarity for ski areas was the fact that the parking lot and lodge were at the top.

By September, about one-third of the expected cost of building the ski area had been raised through stock sales. The foundations for a 1,200-foot-long Hall T-bar was installed, and the trails had been cleared and smoothed. Construction began for the ski lodge but had to be postponed due to a lack of funds. An official opening was held on December 27, and the ski area was on its way to a successful season.

Juniper Hills operated for its first two seasons, 1964–65 and 1965–66, with no lodge, but this was remedied in late 1966 with one if the most modern lodges seen at a ski area of its size. It was patterned after a Swiss chalet, with a roof that extended outward at the corners. Spacious windows overlooked Lake Bonaparte and the ski slopes. Inside the lodge were a ski rental center, a stone fireplace, a snack bar and sitting areas. The lodge would officially be opened in January 1967 and was dedicated to President Verne Wicks for all of his efforts in the development of the area.

More improvements were in store for the 1966–67 season. A new six-hundred-foot-long Hall J-bar serving a short beginner slope was constructed, along with several new trails. This allowed Juniper Hills to become a complete ski area with amenities for all skiers. A new ski patrol, led by Don Grout, was formed with ten National Ski Patrol members. They would help to ensure safe skiing for all and respond immediately to calls for help by skiers.

As Juniper Hills' Ski School developed, a new lead instructor, James Leonard, was hired in 1967. He had previously taught skiing at the Grosstal Ski Slopes in New York. Classes were held on Sundays, and private or semi-private lessons were also available.

A few more improvements were developed for the 1968–69 season. A new $7,000 Thiokol Imp Snow Packer was purchased to help improve the snow quality. One of the trails was widened, and a swampy area near the foot of the T-bar was filled in. Two more instructors, Lea Kachadorian and Charles Bensinger, were brought in to expand the ski school. A new event, the Lollipop Derby, was held on most weekends and was open to children of all ages, allowing them to take part in races that would normally be held for older skiers at other areas. For the 1969–70 season, lights for night skiing were installed.

Juniper Hills, like so many other ski areas, peaked in popularity and usage in the early 1970s. Thereafter, a lack of natural snowfall limited the days of operations for a few seasons into the 1970s. Snowmaking, an expensive addition, was not installed. Financial difficulties grew at the area, and it was forced to close for the 1977–78 season.

It would remain shuttered for that one season before being leased to Paul and Donna Foote, who added several miles of cross-country trails and marketed the lodge to groups outside of skiing for the 1978–79 season. They also added summer campground facilities in 1979, working to expand the facility to near year-round activity. For the 1979–80 season, they added a new trail in the woods near the T-bar and lowered season ticket prices in order to remain competitive.

The Juniper Hills lodge was situated at the top of the ski area, an uncommon characteristic. It featured a protruding roof in the Swiss chalet style. A stone fireplace provided warmth throughout the building, which also housed a snack bar and ski shop. *Courtesy of the Town of Diana Museum, courtesy of Ross Young.*

This undated view of the Juniper Hills ski area shows a few skiers riding up the Hall T-bar. In the background is Lake Bonaparte. Note that scattered trees were left on the slope to provide visual interest. *From the Town of Diana Museum, courtesy of Ross Young.*

This was not enough to save the area. A severe lack of snowfall hit the area hard for the 1979–80 and the 1980–81 seasons, and Juniper Hills was forced to close for good. The base lodge was converted into a home and still stands today.

Visiting the Area

Juniper Hills is completely on private property and cannot be visited. However, the area can be seen from the southeastern shores of Lake Bonaparte. Overhead satellite imagery shows that the majority of the former ski trails are kept clear by the landowner.

Robert Moses State Park

Massena, New York

1969–circa 1973

Seeing the need to increase winter recreational activities, the Thousand Island Park Commission built a rope tow on a gentle slope behind the former Uhl Hall and Rich Office building on the grounds of the Robert Moses State Park. Located nine hundred feet behind the building, the slope also offered tobogganing. Inside the office building, a warming room and first aid offices were set up. Once completed, the tow operated for the first time on January 19, 1969. Skiing was free of charged and was aimed toward children and beginners.

The ski area was in operation for several seasons, with night skiing on weekday nights and daytime skiing on the weekends. By 1973, declining use and the limited scope of this area led to its closure.

Visiting the Area

The former ski area at Robert Moses State Park is open to the public and can be explored, although most of it is grown in. Today, it sits behind the

Nature Center. Pick up a trail map at the office and follow the River Trail behind the Nature Center, which passes through the ski area.

Saint Lawrence State Park

Ogdensburg, New York

Circa 1966–1980

Saint Lawrence State Park first started offering skiing in the mid-1960s, beginning with a rope tow and warming hut. The facilities were fairly basic, but by 1970, plans were announced for a more significant expansion. An "upside-down" ski area, with the parking on the top and views of the Saint Lawrence River and Canada, expected to increase the park's wintertime offerings.

A new master plan was announced for the state park in March 1970, which would greatly expand the existing golf course, as well as the ski area. A new Hall J-bar lift would be the centerpiece of the ski area, with easy grades of 7 to 15 percent. Night skiing was planned to allow skiers from the Ogdensburg area a chance to ski after work. The area would be geared toward beginners and families with mostly easy terrain.

The plan was approved, and work began on the expanded ski area in the fall of 1970. By November, work was nearly 60 percent complete, with a three-story lodge that could accommodate up to seventy persons under construction. Trail work was also nearing completion, with a wide-open slope with scattered tree islands, along with some narrow chutes. The vertical drop on those trails would be quite small, though—only sixty feet, just barely enough to make a few turns before reaching the bottom.

With winter approaching, work was rushed to finish the ski lift and lodge. Finally, the lift opened on January 23, 1971, with free skiing due to the incomplete lodge, which would not be open until the following season. In addition, the lights for night skiing would not be ready until the following season either due to budget cuts. These cuts would affect the area throughout its operation.

For the first several seasons, the ski area was popular, but budget cuts limited the hours to just a few nights and on weekends. At one point in the mid-1970s, volunteers were asked to help run the lift. The final season ended in 1980, after a nearly snowless winter took its final toll.

Visiting the Area

As Saint Lawrence State Park is still in operation, the former ski area can still be visited and explored. From the intersection of Stone Church Road and Route 37, drive north for one-quarter of a mile and turn left into the parking lot. There you can see the lodge that skiers used. Directly north of the parking lot at the top of the area is the building that once housed the engine for the J-bar. As you turn to face the Saint Lawrence River, walk down the old ski slope, which is still clear. In fact, it has been widened in the last decade, which has removed the former lift line and narrow trails. One can walk down seven hundred feet to reach the bottom of the ski area and return via the same route.

Cross-country skiing and sledding is also available. For more information, visit www.nysparks.com.

SEVEN SPRINGS/CLARKSON SEVEN SPRINGS

Parishville, New York

1967–1972, 1975–1990

First developed as a public ski area with the goal of being a year-round major recreational area, the Seven Springs ski area would later be owned by Clarkson College of Technology (and later Clarkson University) for mostly student use. Although it has been closed as a downhill ski area since 1990, the area is now seeing a resurgence and has recently been the location of mountain bike races, as well as used by the Clarkson Outing Club. It is a lost ski area only in the sense that there is no lift-served transportation and not that the area is abandoned.

Seven Springs was developed in 1966 by the former landowner, Worth "Bud" Graham, who at the time was supervising the construction of the library classrooms at the nearby Clarkson University. He planned to develop a $300,000 resort on property he owned in Parishville off Crowley Road. He had already built a lodge on the property but planned to add a ten-acre lake, a ski tow and trails, a motel, hiking trails and bridle paths to make the area a true outdoor recreation center. The area was also advertised as having the potential to bring in $200,000 worth of revenue to surrounding communities.

In 1967, he obtained a $50,000 loan from the First National Bank of Norfolk to begin construction of the ski area. A thirteen-hundred-foot-long T-bar was purchased and installed by manufacturer Sneller, and a wide-open two-hundred-foot vertical slope was cleared. The lodge was improved, and the area was able to open for the 1967–68 season.

Throughout the late 1960s and early 1970s, the area remained a modest development. A rope tow was added to a beginner slope. The Potsdam Jaycees would often hold ski lessons at the area, and snowmobile climbs and motorcycle races were also held. The busiest times at the area were when bands were playing in the lodge. The amount of business generated at the area was limited, and payments on the mortgage fell behind. The area closed at the end of the 1971–72 season and was foreclosed on by the bank in 1974. On October 30 of that year, its assets were purchased by the Small Business Administration, with the hope of selling the property to a qualified buyer.

At an auction in December 1974, Clarkson College purchased the ski area for $55,000, beginning the next phase of the facility's use. The area was expected to be a valuable asset to students, providing a wide array of outdoor recreation. After the completion of the sale, in discussing the role that the ski area would play, Clarkson president Robert A. Plane was quoted as saying:

> *I want to see to it that its use will be toward bringing out the very best in all of our students. I would hope also that we can find ways to use the facility, during Clarkson vacations, for the benefit of Potsdam and area residents.*

Although the college wished to open the ski area for the 1974–75 season, it was in too rough of a shape. Being closed for two and a half years with little maintenance had left the lodge run down, along with the ski trails, which were becoming overgrown. Guy Arnold, the director of Recreation Services at Clarkson, led a team of employees and students to spruce up the area, refurbish the lift and renovate the lodge in 1975.

The ski area reopened for the 1975–76 season with a new name reflecting the ownership change—Clarkson Seven Springs. The National Ski Patrol certified a patrol for the area; all twenty-eight members of the new ski patrol were students. Certified ski instructor Peter Southwick oversaw twenty instructors for the ski school. Students were also able to obtain physical education credits by learning to ski at Seven Springs. Students also operated the lift and helped to run the lodge.

In the first season operated by Clarkson, three thousand tickets were sold, and more plans for improvements were announced for the 1976–77 season. The ski rental shop was expanded and was managed by Mike Casey. The lodge could be rented out to students and groups for just forty-five dollars. Bus transportation was organized, which took students from campus to the ski area, for those who did not have their own cars. Finally, a new trail groomer was purchased to help keep the trails smooth.

A lack of snowfall hit the area hard in 1979 and 1980, with little skiing during those years. While installation of a snowmaking machine was considered, the costs would be too high. Clarkson Seven Springs was entirely reliant on natural snow for the rest of its existence.

In addition to its alpine trails, the ski area was becoming known for its excellent cross-country network. Over ten miles of trails were in place by 1983, which had been maintained and cleared by the recreation department and outing club. The trails were partially groomed and were used by the Clarkson, as well as the St. Lawrence University ski teams for training (once the Snow Bowl was closed). Many cross-country races were held there throughout the 1980s, including the Potsdam Langlauf Cross Country Race.

Despite the benefit of it being an excellent beginner area, Clarkson Seven Springs could never move beyond that. With a limited vertical drop and no true expert terrain, it had little to offer advanced skiers besides a place to make some turns for a few hours. Recreation director Bob Arnold noted in a 1989 interview with the *Clarkson Integrator* that "it's unfortunate most people learn to ski at Seven Springs but then move on to the other mountains like Titus and Big Tupper."

Adding to the woes of decreasing patronage was a lack of natural snowfall in the late 1980s. This drastically reduced the length of the season and further accelerated students to find other, more reliable ski areas that had snowmaking. The ski area closed at the end of the 1989–90 season.

In May 1991, the university made the closure permanent, saving $78,000. For a few years, the cross-country trails were maintained, but the lodge was mothballed. It later burned to the ground. The T-bar lift was removed, its destination unknown.

Although the lift no longer functioned, Seven Springs did not become an abandoned place. It has been used as the location for the university's

Students from Clarkson Seven Springs are seen here on one of the lower slopes of the ski area. In the background, the base lodge and T-bar can be clearly seen. This particular slope was often used for beginner lessons. *Courtesy of the Clarkson University Archives.*

The main slope at Seven Springs is maintained and clear in this October 2014 view. The former T-bar ran up on the left side (looking down) of the slope. Only foundations for this lift remain. The former ski lodge was at the bottom of the slope, also with only foundation remnants.

Winterfest, and in recent years, students have created a network of mountain bike trails, which are frequently used by the outing club. It is still very much an active place for the Clarkson community.

Visiting the Area

Clarkson Seven Springs is owned by the university and is for student use. It is not open to the public.

Clarkson College of Technology Ski Hill

Potsdam, New York

1950–circa mid-1960s

Prior to owning and operating the Seven Springs area, a rope tow facility operated on the campus of Clarkson College (now Clarkson University) of Technology from 1950 until the mid-1960s. It was a relatively small ski area but was quite popular while in operation.

In 1949, the Clarkson-Potsdam State Teachers Outing Club, which had many members interested in skiing, looked into the possibility of building a ski area on campus. After working through an approval process, they were granted the right to develop one on a portion of the Hill Campus. During the summer of 1949, students worked to clear a slope and used heavy equipment to smooth and grade the one-hundred-foot vertical slope. A twenty-meter ski jump with multiple levels was also built, along with a four-hundred-foot-long electric rope tow. A small warming hut was also built, and a ski patrol was set up, to be operated by the club under the supervision of Dick Sitterly.

Once completed, the rope tow first operated in March 1950. Open to the public as well as students, the cost for a day ticket was just fifty cents. Several competitions were held at the facility using the ski jump during the 1950s.

By the late 1950s, use of the hill had subsided, but in 1960, a newly organized ski club was formed to rejuvenate the slope. Student members repaired the tow, cleared the slope of debris (with help from Alpha Phi Omega) and reorganized the ski patrol. The jump would not be repaired until 1963, though even then it was never used. Richard Tuthill, a student at the time, recalls rebuilding the jump:

> I remember rebuilding the jump during the weekend after President Kennedy's assassination. Our group was composed of everyone we could muster who wanted to reestablish skiing as a varsity sport at Clarkson after it had been discontinued in my freshman year, the year before. We never used the jump after we rebuilt it. It was too small and we preferred the jumps at St. Lawrence. St. Lawrence had graciously allowed the Clarkson Ski Team to use their jumps as part of the usage agreement that covered the SLU Snow Bowl.

The Clarkson College of Technology Ski Hill was a wide-open slope with scattered trees, along with a thirty-meter jump. The rope tow can be seen on the far left in this 1952 view. *From the* Clarksonian *1952 Yearbook.*

The ski hill continued to operate until the mid-1960s, when usage declined and new student housing was built on the slope. While skiing ceased temporarily at the college, it later shifted to new area about a decade later—Clarkson Seven Springs.

Visiting the Area

As this is a private university, the area cannot be explored by the public. Today, most of the hill is student housing (Woodstock Village), though a small portion remains of the slope, which is used by students for sledding. The Cora and Bayard Clarkson Science Center is at the top of the hill. There are no remnants of the jump or the tow.

Skyline

Redford, New York

1959–circa 1963

Skyline, a rope tow ski area, operated in Redford from 1959 until around 1962. Owned by Donald Miner and managed by Clarence Alexander, construction on the area began in September 1959. Approximately $5,000 was spent in 1959 to open the ski area—including the construction of an 850-foot-long rope tow, trail clearing, a warming trailer and a 70- by 125-foot ice-skating rink. A parking lot for one hundred cars was also cleared. Skiing would be available on a 160-foot vertical drop on an intermediate slope.

The area opened for business on December 26, 1959, with fresh snow, as well as affordable ticket rates—just $1.50 for adults and $0.50 for children.

Over the next few years, more improvements came to Skyline, including another rope tow and a lodge. In February 1961, the First Annual Giant Slalom competition was held at the area.

In early January 1963, a large ice jam on the Saranac River caused considerable flooding and damage to the base lodge. It is believed that this was the cause of the area closing that season.

Visiting the Area

While the former Skyline Ski Area is on private property (please do not trespass), the area is still visible. From Route 3 in Redford, take Pup Hill Road across the Saranac River. Skyline was located on the hill on the right immediately after you cross the river, behind several homes.

Polar Valley

Saranac, New York

1958–1963

Polar Valley was a family-owned and family-operated ski area located in the town of Saranac. Husband-and-wife team Major Moxie A. and Elizabeth Shirley arrived in the area in 1955; they were originally from Texas. Moxie was assigned to the nearby Plattsburgh Air Force Base as a B-47 aircraft commander, and once they arrived, they fell in love with the region. Seeing the growing ski industry, they decided to build a ski area on their property. Their children, Charles, Don, Ann, Mike and Linda, assisted in the operation.

In the fall of 1958, the family built a rope tow on an open slope (geared toward beginners and intermediates), and the ski area opened on December 21, 1958, with a six-inch base and three inches of new powder. Ticket prices were one dollar for children and three dollars for adults. Ski conditions were mostly decent during that first season, with Polar Valley operating mostly on weekends.

Although the first and second seasons were successful, the 1960–61 season was rough, with little snow, limiting the days of operation. However, during this time, the family began to operate a Christmas tree farm on their property as an extra source of income. Undeterred by the poor season, improvements were made for the 1961–62 season, including a snack bar and night skiing.

The 1962–63 ski season would be the final one for this brief operation, with the exact reason for closure unknown, although it is surmised that the family moved away from the area.

Visiting the Area

Although remnants of the tow were spotted about ten years ago, the author was unable to find them, and there is nothing left of Polar Valley today.

St. Lawrence University Snow Bowl

South Colton, New York

1938–1946 (non-lift-served), 1946–1982 (lift-served)

Few ski areas in the northern Adirondacks can match the history of the St. Lawrence University Snow Bowl. From serving as a training area for students, to hosting region-wide intercollegiate alpine and Nordic championships, to hosting world-class ski jumpers and coaches, the area was a historically important ski center. In its later years, after the ski area closed, it was used by students for their annual Snow Bowl Party, which attracted hundreds of revelers. Today, the area is abandoned and returning back to nature, though still visible.

The St. Lawrence University (SLU) Ski Team was organized in 1932 and participated in regional competitions throughout the 1930s, including at the Dartmouth Winter Carnival in 1932. It held its own winter carnival two years later. However, the ski team was looking for a more challenging location that could be used to develop and grow its ski program. According to Adam Terko, assistant nordic ski coach at SLU, who has extensively researched the Snow Bowl, the slope was discovered by students on the way back from a trip to New England. They had noticed the steep slope behind Cold River and began to make some runs, but the owner was not too pleased with their visit.

A few years later, though, the landowner was more receptive to students using the slope, and through the efforts of Coach James Littlejohn and Roy Clogston, the area was leased from the owner, with a five-year lease issued in 1941. The area, a large bowl-shaped slope behind the farm, was a perfect spot for a ski area. Located in a shielded valley, the area was eight hundred feet higher than campus and faced north. The slopes needed little clearing, as they were already wide open. In December 1938, Otto Schniebs toured the area and declared it to be "more satisfactory than the one used by the Dartmouth University Students at Hanover."

On January 21, 1939, the center hosted its first intercollegiate ski meet, with teams from Clarkson, Hamilton, Union and SLU all participating. Events included a four-mile cross-country race and a slalom.

During World War II, the area was open only sporadically. Wartime restrictions limiting the use of gasoline made the university cancel transportation to the area. But once the war ended, the Snow Bowl would see a dramatic comeback.

134

Beginning around 1946, the university made a concerted effort to grow and develop its winter sports program. A rope tow—purchased from Thomas Cantwell of Saranac Lake, who had operated Betters Hill—was installed to provide uphill transportation. In January 1947, a four-day winter carnival was held, with many events at the Bowl. Additional improvements came for the 1947–48 season. Funded by the Alumni Fund, a new forty-meter jump was carved out of the forest at the northwest end of the area. The Garvey Lumber Company employed James Simone and Ralph Currier to clear the trees and to create the landing area as well. The jump would be one of the finest in the eastern United States. The slalom slope was also extended to the top, with a new trail at the summit to connect the slalom slope to the ski jump. Another rope tow was added to parallel the first, with yet another additional one in 1949, giving the area three lifts.

Perhaps the biggest improvement to the Snow Bowl occurred in late 1947, when Otto Schniebs was promoted to a ski coach. He had already worked with the university in an advisory capacity since 1940 and had helped guide the ski team to four consecutive New York State intercollegiate ski meets from 1942 to 1946. His goals were not only to develop world-class athletes but to also develop a love of skiing for all students. Over the next decade, he would bring much success to the St. Lawrence ski teams as well as to the Snow Bowl. He would retire from ski coaching at St. Lawrence following the end of the 1956–57 season.

In early 1948, manager John Simone outfitted the Snow Bowl with twenty-two thousand watts of lighting, enough to cover twelve acres of skiing. This allowed for more hours of skiing after class and for the outing club and ski teams to have time to practice in the evening. Around this time, a snack bar and warming hut were opened across Route 56, as land was limited near the parking lot and was occasionally flooded due to the Cold River.

Throughout the late 1940s and early 1950s, the Winter Carnival was the main event at the Snow Bowl each year, carrying on the tradition set a decade earlier. These carnivals grew in size with dozens of ski teams attending, participating in ski jumping, slalom and downhill racing and cross-country racing. Adequate snowfall was sometimes limited during that time, and for the 1951 carnival, students held a "snow revival" on campus to "scare away the bad snow conditions that had prevailed over the last three years."

While cutting a new trail for a cross-country event on January 15, 1950, Otto Schniebs and five students became lost in the woods a few miles from the Snow Bowl. Taking the proper precaution to stay in place when lost, they built campfires to stay warm. A rescue team led by Coach Littlejohn found them at 10:00 p.m., no worse for the wear.

A skier poses against the Snow Bowl sign on Route 56 in this promotional photo. In the 1950s, the area featured two rope tows, a wide-open slope, ski jumping and a snack bar (across the street, behind the photo). *Courtesy of the Special Collections, St. Lawrence University Libraries, Canton, New York.*

Otto Schniebs was a longtime coach of Saint Lawrence and was affiliated with the university for seventeen years. He is pictured here on the right with members of the ski team in the 1950s. The sixty-meter jump is in the background. *Courtesy of the Special Collections, St. Lawrence University Libraries, Canton, New York.*

A view of the lower slalom slope of the Snow Bowl. Visible is the engine house for the dual rope tows, as well as the snack bar across the street. The ski bridge connecting the parking lot to the ski area itself can be seen.

In the 1950s, the Saint Lawrence Snow Bowl was served by two parallel rope tows that took skiers to the top of the slalom slope. Lines for the lift would often grow to dozens of skiers. Note the sixty-meter jump on the right, along with the bridge in the foreground that took skiers over the Cold Brook. *Courtesy of the Special Collections, St. Lawrence University Libraries, Canton, New York.*

For the 1950–51 season, a larger sixty-meter jump had been built, making the facility the largest university-operated center in the country. To open the jump on January 14, 1951, famous jumpers Art Devlin and former Olympian Art Tokle were brought in for a ski meet competition. Five hundred fans and student were on hand to see the competition. For the first attempt, both men jumped 160 feet. For the second, Devlin jumped 177 feet, using his "floating takeoff," but Tokle ended up the victor, jumping 182 feet. Even though the competition was over, the two decided to jump one more time to set an unofficial record—this time, Devlin tied Tokle's record, but Tokle was able to beat his own, at 186 feet. One mother in attendance was so wowed by the competition that she told her son, "One day you'll be able to say you were here to witness this."

There were grand plans to repeat this performance the following year; unfortunately, a rainstorm washed away all of the snow and turned the landing area of the jump into a pond. In 1956, at the ski meet, Devlin ended up setting an official record of 184 feet.

Although the area had been open mainly for students and visiting ski teams from its conception until the late 1950s, by 1958, the area had begun to be open to the public on a limited basis. By 1961, the area was open to the public on a more regular basis, with affordable tickets at just one dollar. An advertisement from that period indicated that the snow was packed by rollers for better skiing, an improvement over the manual packing done by students in years prior.

Efforts to modernize the area continue throughout the early 1960s. A one-thousand-foot-long second-hand electric T-bar (from an area in Northern California) was installed for the 1961–62 season by construction firm Fisher and Rexford, replacing the two parallel rope tows and allowing for easier access to the summit. At a cost of $26,000, it was the most expensive improvement in the history of the Snow Bowl. New beginner trails were added to provide variety for all levels of skiing. A new twenty-meter jump was built to supplement the existing forty- and sixty-meter jumps, which were also upgraded.

From the late 1950s through the mid-1960s, a new crop of successful skiers moved through the St. Lawrence ranks, including David Jacobs and C.B. Vaughan. Both were world-class athletes who trained at the Snow Bowl and would move on to have large impacts on the ski industry. David Jacobs later founded Spyder, one of the world's largest manufacturers of clothing for skiers and racers. After his time at St. Lawrence, Vaughan went on to set the world record speed on a downhill run—at an astounding 106 miles per hour. He would also go on to found C.B. Sports, a premier outerwear

Huge crowds turned out for the various jumping competitions held at the Snow Bowl. In this undated but likely early 1950s view, spectators line the edge of the forty- and sixty-meter jumps and wait for jumpers to soar through the air. Note the line of parked cars on Route 56 stretching as far as the eye can see.

This T-bar lift was a major improvement at the Snow Bowl, replacing the dual rope tows. In addition to increasing capacity, the new lift was much easier to ride. *Courtesy of the Special Collections, St. Lawrence University Libraries, Canton, New York.*

Ski team member C.B. Vaughan Jr. negotiates a gate during a race. Vaughn later set a downhill speed record of 106 miles per hour in Portillo, Chile, and founded the C.B. Sports Company. *Courtesy of the Special Collections, St. Lawrence University Libraries, Canton, New York.*

company that is still in business today, although Vaughan has moved on to other ventures.

Vaughan has fond memories of training at the Snow Bowl. He remembers that the slalom slope, while short, was perfect for practice. He would often set up gates on the landing area for the sixty-meter jump, as its steep pitch was also excellent for training.

In 1963, the university promoted ski coach Bob Axtell to be the new chief of operations at the Snow Bowl. He had previously worked as a ski coach at Norwich University and would continue his role as the varsity and freshman ski team coach at St. Lawrence. In 1965, he worked hard to allow the facility to once again host the Eastern Intercollegiate Ski Association, but a lack of snowfall resulted in the event moving to Middlebury, Vermont. Axtell remembers that having the T-bar allowed jumpers to make far more runs per day than if they had to climb the jump themselves, often fifteen to twenty

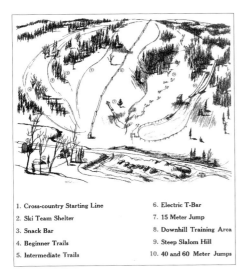

1. Cross-country Starting Line
2. Ski Team Shelter
3. Snack Bar
4. Beginner Trails
5. Intermediate Trails
6. Electric T-Bar
7. 15 Meter Jump
8. Downhill Training Area
9. Steep Slalom Hill
10. 40 and 60 Meter Jumps

An undated but likely early 1960s trail map shows the layout of the ski area. From left to right were beginner trails, the T-bar and intermediate (slalom) slope, a fifteen-meter jump, a steeper slalom slope and the forty- and sixty-meter jumps. *Courtesy of the Special Collections, St. Lawrence University Libraries, Canton, New York.*

jumps instead of five to six at other training facilities.

By the late 1960s, the Snow Bowl had moved past its peak, as ski jumping was waning as a widespread sport, and other areas were developing such as Whiteface and Big Tupper. Rumblings about closing the facility began in 1970, as the university started selling some land on Catamount Mountain. In 1972, Bob Axtell was moved back to being a ski coach, effectively leaving nobody to manage the ski area. By 1974, a report by vice-president of student affairs Peter E. Van de Water outlined the issues affecting the Snow Bowl.

In his report, a lack of recent snowfall was noted as limiting operations, resulting in a deficit of $20,000. Days of operation had fallen to only thirty-one in 1973, as opposed to the late 1960s, when up to ninety days of skiing were recorded. There was no dedicated beginner area. The snack bar was located across the street, requiring one to remove his or her skis and walk across Route 56, and the snack bar offered only food from vending machines. There was also a lack of any effort to attract new skiers or to promote the area.

In the same report, recommendations for improvements to the area were explored, which included moving the snack bar to near the parking lot, adding a second T-bar lift to increase capacity, restoring lights for night skiing (which were no longer operational), adding snowmaking, adding a beginner tow and expanding the cross-country network. This five-year plan would cost $130,000.

Unfortunately, due to the high cost and potential lack of return, none of these improvements was implemented. The area limped along for another eight years and finally closed at the end of the 1981–82 season. The T-bar was removed, and the old snack bar began to decay across the street. Despite its closure, the area was still owned by the university until 2004, when it was sold. Students continued to use the property, including the old ski jump site, for winter parties, attended by hundreds of students.

Visiting the Area

Today, the Snow Bowl is not accessible to the public and is on private property. However, it is easily visible from Route 56, and there is a New York State fishing area at the foot of the area, on the Cold River. Land beyond the river is not open to the public. From the parking lot, located about two miles south of the center of South Colton on Route 56, face the ski area. On the left is the main slalom slope, still visible but becoming overgrown. On the right is the ski jump—take time to imagine what it must have been like to soar off that jump.

Behind you and across the street is the former snack bar. This, too, is on private property but can be examined from a distance by walking along the road.

CLIFTON-FINE LIONS CLUB

Star Lake, New York

1950–1972

In 1950, seeing the growth of skiing across the northern Adirondacks, the Clifton-Fine Lions Club decided to build its own area. It would be completely free to children and would operate for over twenty years before declining use took its toll.

A suitable location was located behind the Twin Lakes Hotel, where several interesting hills with good exposures existed. Although the vertical would not be substantial, just a little over one hundred feet, some steep sections of up to 30 percent grades would be possible. In addition, the location had the benefit of being right in Star Lake, a short distance from the Clifton-Fine School, with parking available near the hotel. It was hoped that this proximity would provide the necessary usage to maintain a ski area.

In September 1950, the Lions Club set up a ski committee, headed by Carl Djuvik, which was charged with raising funds and finding volunteer labor to clear the slopes. To raise funds, a season ticket rate of ten dollars for adults was set. Work progressed during the fall, and by December, it was nearly complete. As an engineer, Djiwick was able to rig up a safety gate for the tow and would later build three more of them, including a ski jump.

The Clifton-Fine Lions Club often hosted ski meets for children. Here, a young skier navigates some gates on the racecourse. One of the rope tows is visible in the background. *By Ken Ross, courtesy of Lyman Ross.*

The ski area thrived in those first few seasons. Fundraisers and meetings were also held, including one in 1953, when athletic trainer and ski enthusiast Doc Littlejohn from St. Lawrence University visited and praised the facilities.

Throughout the rest of the 1950s and into the 1960s, the ski area was truly at its peak. On most weekends and holidays, several volunteers from the Clifton-Fine Lions Club oversaw the operations and made sure nobody got hurt. Lessons were given free of charge to children by Lions Club members. Ski meets were popular and were often planned by Ken Ross and Carl Djiwick.

Lyman Ross, the son of Ken Ross and who learned to ski at this area, shares his memories of skiing in the 1960s:

> *The warming shack and the tow motor were at the top of the bunny hill. A second tow took you to the top of the main slope, which was on the other side of the hill. A third tow went from the bottom of the main slope to the top. At the bottom of the main slope there was a short, flat trail that led to the flank of the hill where a fourth tow brought you back to the middle of the hill, where the warming shack and tow motor were located.*

Here, skiers enjoy a run in fresh powder from the top of one of the rope tows of the Clifton-Fine Lions Club ski area. The club operated four rope tows, all powered by the same engine. *By Ken Ross, courtesy of Lyman Ross.*

A small building served as the "base lodge" but was known locally as the "shack." At some point in the 1960s, a large, round fire pit with a funnel-shaped metal hood/chimney was installed and gave it a more cosmopolitan air. There was night skiing and an old PA system that was sometimes used to broadcast music to the slopes. As I recall, the music included Swiss yodeling and other such alpine themes.

The rope tows made a big impression on me as a kid. My biggest fear was to get halfway up the hill and to start sliding backward as the rope sped through my hands. This usually happened late in the day as you began to tire and rope and mittens got icy. It wasn't unusual for someone to slide backward and take out several other skiers. The only way to avoid this was to drop and roll, but if you weren't fast enough, it was easy to end up with one ski on the opposite side of the rope, which was now dragging across your ankle. One tow was on an especially steep slope and served a seldom used and out-of-way portion of the hill. The rope dragged heavily on the ground creating a deep groove in the snow, and it was almost impossible for us kids to get up this slope unless we were either in a group or with an adult. A large splice on the rope was known as the "hot dog," and we raced around the hill trying to catch it.

Like at many small ski areas in the early 1970s, usage of the tow began to dwindle, and by 1972, the Lions Club had decided to close the ski area. Students from the nearby school had moved on to bigger areas, such as Big Tupper.

Visiting the Area

There are several remnants of the ski area that remain. The area can be accessed from the Clifton-Fine Municipal Golf Course when the golf course is closed. From Route 3, face the golf course and take the fairway on the far left for about one thousand feet behind the ice arena. There will be a trail through the woods. Follow the trail for a short distance until you reach the former ski area. There are still quite a few remnants of the rope tow scattered in the woods.

INDIAN RIVER

Theresa, New York

Late 1940s

In the late 1940s, a small rope tow ski area named Indian River operated in Theresa. It was quite small, and featured only a fifty-foot drop. A three-hundred-foot-long rope tow served two slopes, the East and the West. It operated weekends only and charged fifty cents for the day.

This area was more than likely a personal or family tow that was open to the public. There are very few references to its existence. It likely closed due to its isolated location and small size.

Visiting the Area

The 1949 *Ski New York Guidebook* listed the area as being on the "County Road" one mile to the east of Theresa. There are several small hills in that region that could have been the Indian River area, but it is unknown which of them is and, thus, if there are any remnants.

V

Lost Ski Areas of the Champlain Valley Region

Although the Champlain Valley region of the northern Adirondacks was not particularly known as a skiing destination, five formerly operating ski areas have become lost in this region. Most were small, community ski areas, and none of the lost areas ever offered more than a rope tow.

The first lost area in this region was Rand Hill, near Beekmantown. Operated by the Plattsburgh Ski Club, it was open for a few years prior to World War II. Its distance away from Plattsburgh itself, in an era when most did not have cars, prevented the area from succeeding. The lift fell into disrepair during the war, and various attempts at reopening it afterward failed. Another brief operation was Hill 13, which operated for only one year in the late 1940s, likely closing due to its isolated location.

One of the longer-lasting areas was the Baldpate Ski Club in Crown Point. It was a ski center dedicated to teaching young people the sport, and it operated for nearly ten years before falling into disuse.

The longest-operating lost ski area was at the Plattsburg Air Force Base Golf Course, where a rope tow operated for over two decades, primarily for those stationed at the base. Today, portions of its rope tow remain standing, a testament to its operation.

Rand Hill

Beekmantown, New York

1940–1943 (lift-served), 1946–1950 (non-lift-served)

In 1937, the Plattsburgh Ski Club was formed with an initial six members to promote the sport among area residents. At first, the club enjoyed ski areas in North Creek, Ticonderoga and Lake Placid, but by the following year, there was a strong push to develop its own ski area. The cost of travel was too much for local residents, and a skiing area closer to home was needed. One such location was found in the summer and fall of 1938, at the foot of Rand Hill near Beekmantown, where the club built a one-half-mile-long ski run. The location was chosen because it was over one thousand feet higher in elevation than Plattsburgh with significantly more snow. The club quickly secured a fifteen-year lease and started plans for a much larger development.

By 1940, the area had expanded to include ten miles of cross-country trails (built on long-abandoned logging trails), a ski shelter and a wide variety of open slopes. During this time, the club also changed its name to the Winter Sports Club of Plattsburgh in order to showcase that it was about more than just skiing. One thing was still missing from its slopes—a rope tow—and plans were set into motion in late 1939 to reach this goal.

In early 1940, a rope tow was finally constructed at the new development and opened by mid-February. The area was an instant hit, and hundreds were soon enjoying the slopes. Membership in the club also grew during this time to over two hundred—and with an annual fee of one dollar, who could pass it up?

Transportation to the area could be difficult, as not all club members owned vehicles. For the 1940–41 season, carpools were set up to alleviate this problem.

More improvements were in store for the new season. The new lunch counter was described in a *Plattsburgh Daily Press* article:

> *The new facilities include a lunch counter in the club's cabin. Here, caterers serve hot dogs and hamburger sandwiches, and steaming coffee and chocolate. This innovation last Sunday was acclaimed by the skiers as a real service, especially when mercury is at zero or lower.*

After yet another successful season, club members, during the summer of 1941, worked hard to improve the slope and clear the brush from the trails, with work parties behind on the slope. The club also developed a program during this time to teach skiing to area children, who could learn for free, with the eventual hope that they would join the club. Ski teams were invited to use the slopes for the 1941–42 season.

Changes were in store for the 1942–43 season. With World War II in progress, the area changed its goals, emphasizing itself as a physical fitness area for potential servicemen and as a leisure center to reduce stress for area workers. As the war continued, the ability to operate a ski area became too difficult for the club, and the area was forced to close. The tow sat idle for the next several years and became inoperable.

Several attempts were made at reopening the area once the war concluded. In late 1946, the club reorganized and brought in Ron McKenzie of Lake Placid to speak about how the club could be a success again. Skiers did return to the slopes in the late 1940s, enjoying the area and the ski cabin, but the tow was in significant need of repair. Trying to hedge its bets, the club assisted Champlain College in developing a small ski slope at Hill 13 in Peasleeville in 1947, but that operation was brief and closed by 1949. The club had folded by 1950, ending any chance of reopening the lift. It was a little less than a decade later before a similar ski area, Beartown, was developed nearby to fill the void of Rand Hill.

Visiting the Area

The ski area was located on Rand Hill, on slopes behind the current Beartown Ski Area (but not part of it), although the exact location is vague. It is doubtful that there are any remnants left.

Baldpate Ski Club

Crown Point, New York

1952–circa 1963

Located in the Ironville section of Crown Point, the Baldpate Ski Club area was a rope tow area that lasted for just over a decade. It opened in 1952 and featured a base lodge with a fireplace that served as a hub for club meetings. Gerald Abbott, who used to ski there with his family, helped clear the slopes in the early 1950s. According to Clark Burrows, there was a large main slope with a side trail on the left as one faced the hill, with the tow powered by an old pickup truck. A second tow section extended above the first, to provide additional vertical. In addition, a beginner's slope had its

Baldpate's main ski slope was served by the rope tow on the right and featured scattered gladed sections for skiers to enjoy. To the left (not pictured) were a few additional trails, and to the right, above the first tow, was another lift section. The young skier at the bottom of the photo making her way toward the lift is Stephanie Abbott, with Terry Abbott in the lift line. *By Gerald Abbott, courtesy of the Ticonderoga Historical Society.*

own tow. He remembers that members had to help pack the slope manually before the area could operate.

Although the tow was enjoyed by club members, it was founded mostly as a youth activity project by the town board and state youth commission, to encourage outdoor recreation and healthful activities. It operated on weekends and holidays. Various student meets were held on the hill with local high school students. In the fall, work parties with many student volunteers were held to help clear the slope of summer growth and string up the rope tow for the following season.

It appears that the area ceased to operate after 1963, and it was left to return to forest. While the exact reason for closure is unknown, it is likely that decreasing membership and the growth of nearby larger ski areas led to its demise.

Visiting the Area

The Baldpate Ski Club area was located on Old Furnace Road and is now indistinguishable from nearby terrain. No known remnants exist.

Hill 13 on Terry Mountain

Peasleeville, New York

1948–1949

A brief ski area, Hill 13 was a joint venture between the Champlain College Outing Club and the Winter Sports Club of Plattsburgh. Built on Terry Mountain, it was named Hill 13 as it was thirteen miles from Plattsburgh. The two groups collaborated to build a 645-foot-long tow on a slope with a vertical drop of 126 feet. College students provided the bulk of the manpower to build the area. The slope was gentle and was geared mainly toward beginners.

The tow was put into operation in early 1948 but was used only sporadically for that first season. It was used on occasion until the end of the 1949, then appears to have closed. The exact reason for its closure is unknown, but the Winter Sports Club closing and the relative distance of the slope from the college (where few students owned cars) likely were the reasons.

Visiting the Area

Hill 13 was located on a slope on Terry Mountain one mile east of Peasleeville. There appears to be nothing left of this very brief development.

Plattsburgh Air Force Base Golf Club

Plattsburgh, New York

1968–early 1980s

A small beginner ski area once operated on the property of the Plattsburgh Air Force Base Golf Club, for about fifteen years. It was primarily used by those stationed at the base, as well as their families.

In the fall of 1968, the Recreation Services Department for the base was looking to develop winter recreation on-site. A "resort" was developed, with a focus on downhill skiing. The 380th Civil Engineering built a rope tow on a short seventy-five-foot vertical slope adjacent to the golf club. Complete with night skiing, the area was the perfect spot for skiers to learn the sport, especially considering that many of those assigned to the base were non-skiers.

The area operated for about fifteen years, until the early 1980s. The exact reason for its closure is unknown, but it is likely that decreasing usage, combined with a lack of consistent snowfall (the area is only at 140 feet above sea level), led to its demise.

Visiting the Area

Although the ski area is no longer operating, the golf course is—now known as the Barracks Golf Course—and is open to the public. The former ski slope is located a short distance behind the Pro Shop, and several remnants exist. Several towers for the rope tow are still standing, including some light fixtures. At the top of the lift, some fencing remains. The most substantial remnant is the former housing for the rope tow at the top, though this is slowly collapsing.

A visit to the former ski area is best enjoyed after a round of golf. If you are going to check out the area, please visit the pro shop first to let

The former ski slope at the Plattsburgh Air Force Base Golf Club is still recognizable in this view, about halfway from the bottom. Note the rope tow lift towers on the left, with attached pulleys and lights. The slope was quite gentle and was geared toward beginners. *Courtesy of Kevin Papenfuss.*

them know that you will be on the property. For more information on the Barracks, please visit www.thebarracksgolf.com.

Blue Boar Ski Center

Willsboro, New York

1964–1977

The Blue Boar Ski Center was a rope tow area that operated as part of the Camp Pok-O-Moonshine Winter Week, from 1964 until around 1977. Named after a legendary ogre of nearby Long Pond, this tow was not open to the general public but rather for student campers during the Christmas holiday week each year. Camp director and owner Jack Swan and his father, Colonel H.T. Swan, obtained a 450-foot-long rope tow from the former

Whiteface/Marble Mountain Ski Area in Wilmington. He remembers that the truck that brought the tow to Blue Boar was so heavy it was barely one inch above the pavement.

The slope was cleared in the fall of 1964 at the farmhouse that served as headquarters for the camp's Winter Week, the former Smith Farm, later known as Beaverbrook Farm on Carver Road. During the first week in the 1964–65 season, there was no snow—and the sixteen campers ended up playing football on the slope instead. A few days into the camp, almost a foot of snow fell, and the rope tow was put into action. Besides skiing, campers could enjoy tobogganing, skating, trips to Whiteface and Paleface ski areas and other local activities.

Throughout the rest of the 1960s until about 1977, the tow was operated during the Winter Week but remained only a small part of the overall activities. Lights were installed for night tobogganing. According to Jack Swan, the slope was being used more and more for sledding and not skiing. Most campers preferred the day trips to Whiteface or Paleface. By 1977, the decision was made to move the week to the camp's property on Long Pond, and a handle tow for tubing was installed and is still used to this day.

Visiting the Area

Located on Carver Road, the area is on private property today and cannot be explored. The rope tow no longer stands on the property. For more information on Camp Pok-O-Moonshine, now known as Camp Pok-O-MacCready Camps, visit www.pokomac.com.

VI

Restored Ski Areas of the Northern Adirondacks

Occasionally, a ski area that has been lost for a long amount of time comes back to life. It is not a common occurrence—once a ski area closes, a comeback is rare. Often, the lifts are sold and removed, equipment like groomers and snowmaking are sold off to pay debts and base lodges are vandalized. The property can also be sold off to developers for other purposes. If an area can be saved, it is typically due to the dedication of its owners and/or volunteers, who often must spend a considerable amount of money and time to rebuild. This occurred with the two cases described here.

Big Tupper in Tupper Lake had been lost for nearly a decade before ARISE volunteers refurbished the mountain in 2009. This involved extensive clearing of overgrown ski trails, lift engineering and maintenance and reopening the base lodge. While the reopening of Big Tupper has not been easy, the groundwork is laid for its continued restoration.

Otis Mountain in Elizabethtown was lost for nearly sixteen years when owner Jeff Allott purchased the property and reopened it as a semi-private ski area. Years of work by him, his family and friends have made the property viable again, both for skiing and for music festivals. Future plans include developing a co-operative, which might operate the ski area for the public.

Could other areas come back? It is doubtful—many have been lost for so long that there is very little infrastructure left. A few areas, like Paleface, are mostly intact but are now private estates. Other locations have virtually disappeared into the Adirondack landscape, having been closed for over seventy years.

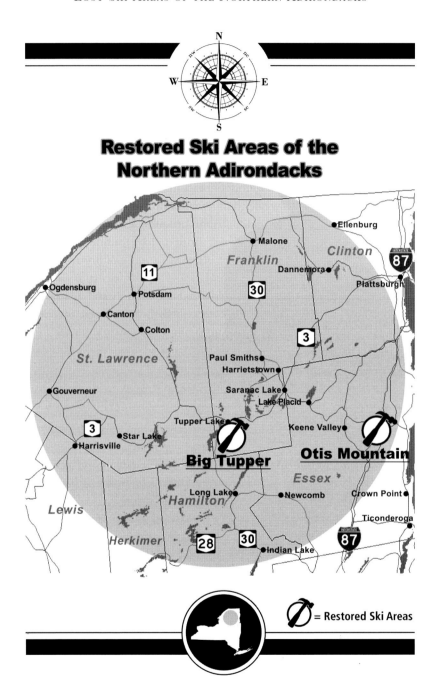

Only two ski areas with lengthy closures have reopened—Big Tupper in Tupper Lake and Otis Mountain in Elizabethtown. Big Tupper is open to the public, while Otis Mountain is a semi-private ski area. *Courtesy of Brandon Capasso.*

BIG TUPPER

Tupper Lake, New York

1960–1999, 2009–Present

Big Tupper, located on Mount Morris, one of New York State's largest privately owned ski areas, is currently in the midst of a slow but steady restoration of its former stature. Its history has been filled with high and low points, and the mere fact that it has survived into the present day is a testament to the community support it receives. Its revitalization is an example of what can be accomplished when a dedicated group of citizens work hard to save a local asset.

The history of Big Tupper is long and extensive, being such a large ski area that opened over fifty years ago. An entire book could certainly be written about it. This section attempts to give an overview of the history of the mountain, its abandonment and its restoration.

Big Tupper's story begins with Sugar Loaf, the rope tow ski area located just a short distance away from the present ski area. Sugar Loaf had introduced residents to the sport for decades, and without it, Big Tupper would never have opened.

Although Sugar Loaf reopened in the late 1950s, after being closed for many years, attention quickly turned to the larger Mount Morris just behind the area. Developing the mountain into a ski area had been casually discussed before, but it was not until 1956 when it was seriously considered. At that time, according to a 1959 report commissioned by the Mount Morris Development Committee, Otto Schniebs was asked to inspect the mountain to see if it could be developed into a ski center. His field study proved that indeed it was suitable. Sel Hannah (of Franconia, New Hampshire) and Sidney Cox completed two more field studies, in 1957 and 1958, complete with designs for trails and lifts.

Then, according to the 1958 report, the Mount Morris Development Committee was organized, composed of members of the village and town boards, the Winter Sports Club, the local chamber of commerce and concerned citizens in order to begin to plan for its development. Plans solidified by 1959, including a new access road, a double chairlift and a T-bar lift to serve a vertical drop of 760 feet, night skiing and half a dozen trails to start, with the potential for many more. It was hoped that the area would attract college students, visitors and locals alike to enjoy what would be the second largest ski area in the Adirondack State Park, behind Whiteface.

Following the planning, the Town of Altamont Board enacted several resolutions to authorize a bond for $465,000 for the construction of a ski area on Mount Morris, on land leased from the Oval Wood Dish Company. A name was selected for the development—Big Tupper—just before the resolution was put before voters. Voters had the final say, and on June 3, 1960, the resolution was passed, but not overwhelmingly—455 in favor to 359 opposed. Immediately, bids were set out for the construction of the access road, lodge, ski trails and lifts. The Beaudette Construction Company won the bid for the road, the Upstate Logging Company won the bid for the trail clearing and Hall Ski Lifts of Watertown, New York, won the bid for the T-bar and chairlift with a midstation. Work began in July 1960, with all companies working at the same time. In addition, the former rope tow and ski hut from Sugar Loaf was brought up the mountain, with the tow to serve a beginner section.

In October 1960, Don Adams was hired for the general manager position, as he had been involved in the planning project for the past few years. Paul Brown, a well-known ski instructor, was hired to operate the new ski school. A strong publicity campaign began during that month, advertising the new ski area in local and regional publications and through various media outlets.

After the frenetic summer and fall, the ski area was all set to open in late December. Despite poor snow conditions, over one thousand skiers tested the mountain on December 26, 1960, and gave it rave reviews. A formal dedication and extravaganza was held on January 28, 1961, with many dignitaries in attendance, various parades, music and additional celebrations. Clearly, Big Tupper was an exciting development in Tupper Lake, and its future appeared bright. The chairlift was operated during the summer, allowing visitors the chance to see the spectacular scenery.

Although the first season went well, the following one saw little snow, and Big Tupper had closed by the end of February. By 1962, the area was not bringing in the expected income to help pay for the large debt incurred by the town, but this was partially due to poor snowfall. The access road had also turned to muck during the spring and had extensive work performed on it in 1962 to improve access. Paving would not occur until 1964.

Throughout the rest of the 1960s, additional improvements were made at Big Tupper. New trails were added from both the top of the chairlift and T-bar, along with additional night skiing terrain. Some seasons, like 1965–66, were so snowy that Big Tupper became the last ski area in the state to close. In

In the 1960s, Big Tupper had three sections, as shown in this panorama—a rope tow–served beginner slope on the far left, Chair 1 in the center and the T-bar trails at the far right.

A 1971 view of the Big Tupper base lodge prior to its later expansion. Its chalet design provided expansive views of the ski area. In the background is Chair 1, the first chairlift on the mountain. *By Ken Ross, courtesy of Lyman Ross.*

158

1968, it opened on November 16 due to extensive natural snowfall, the earliest in its history. In the late 1960s, a Mitey Mite surface lift was installed near the T-bar, which resulted in the closure of the rope tow.

Setbacks hit the area in the early 1970s, including a fire started by lightning that destroyed the base of the chairlift on July 24, 1971, and another fire that destroyed the ski patrol and first aid building on December 10, 1973. Although repairs were expensive, both facilities were quickly repaired or replaced.

In its first decade, skiing visits had improved from 7,462 for the 1960–61 season to 48,411 for the 1970–71 season. Growth began to plateau in the early 1970s, and the ski area had essentially reached its full capacity. Seeking to expand with an additional chairlift, new manager Edgar Fletcher found one at the Duchess Mountain Ski Area in Beacon, an abandoned project. The chair, installed at Duchess Mountain in 1970 and operated for only fifty hours, was in pristine shape. In 1975, the Town of Altamont approved a bond for $125,000 to purchase and move the chairlift. Installed during the summer of 1975, parallel to the T-bar, the new chair, called Chair 2, expanded lift capacity and accessed new trails. The bond also provided funding for a lodge expansion of four thousand square feet in 1976, which relieved overcrowding in the original lodge.

The final major lift expansion at Big Tupper came in the summer of 1978, with the addition of another double chairlift, Chair 3, which went almost to the summit of Mount Morris. More trails, to be used by the new lift, were cut, which also expanded the area's vertical drop to over 1,100 feet, making it one of the largest in the state. The trail count was boosted to twenty-four with the new lift. In 1979, a new midstation was added to the original Chair 1, which allowed less-experienced skiers the chance to enjoy the lower slopes.

As the decade of the 1980s approached, Big Tupper seemed poised for great success. However, the reality was somewhat different. The hopes of a boost of skiers from the 1980 Winter Olympics in Lake Placid were dashed because snowfall was nonexistent. The new summit chairlift hardly operated during this timeframe due to the lack of snowfall. Calls for snowmaking were insistent, and a system was put in place by 1984.

By the mid-1980s, the Town of Altamont, burdened with debt from the ski area, began to look at all options for the facility, from closing it, to having ORDA (the Olympic Regional Development Authority) take over, to selling to a private buyer.

In 1986, bids were put out to sell the ski area, and Roger Jakubowski had the highest bid, at $550,000. Jakubowski had made millions with various businesses in Atlantic City, New Jersey, and had been purchasing various properties in the Adirondacks. He owned the ski area until 1992, though Pat Cunningham operated it for a few years in the late 1980s. Jakubowski was regarded as a controversial owner. On one hand, he did save the ski area from closure, but on the other, he made unpopular changes, such as removing water fountains to increase drink sales at the snack bar. Little money was invested in the mountain during this time, and by 1992, it was in poor shape. Jakubowski stopped making payments on the mountain, and Big Tupper was soon foreclosed on.

While this situation is common among many lost ski areas, Big Tupper got another chance from Peter Day and Leroy Pickering, who were able to purchase the area at an auction for $310,000. The two owners invested over $1 million to bring Big Tupper up to a satisfactory condition, including reopening Chair 3, which had not run for three years due to neglect. The owners focused on snowmaking improvements, with nearly 100 percent coverage completed by 1995. Once again, it seemed that Big Tupper had escaped closure and would succeed.

The winters of the late 1990s were not kind to Big Tupper, or to other areas, with warm temperatures and reduced natural snowfall. Snowmaking on all trails was expensive, and what snow was made was frequently washed out. The ski area was losing over $300,000 every year with no end in sight. Day and Pickering had reached the end of what they could do to save the ski area, and it closed at the end of 1999.

The closing hit the community hard. Despite all of its financial troubles, Big Tupper was a major asset in town, providing employment to locals, serving as a location for outdoor recreation and as a draw for tourists. Generations of kids had learned to ski at the area. Now, there would be no more local skiing, and skiers would have to move on to other, more distant mountains.

Although the owners had considered selling off the valuable assets of the ski area, most of the infrastructure remained. Throughout the 2000s, vandalism and deterioration took its toll on the property, but the fact that the lifts and lodge remained was instrumental in saving the area. Had the lifts been removed, or the lodge burned, the chances of renewal would have been nearly impossible.

There were many attempts at renewing the area on an all-volunteer or co-operative basis throughout the first decade of the 2000s, but none was successful. This began to change in 2004, when a development corporation, the Adirondack Club Resort, purchased the ski area and surrounding land, totaling seven thousand acres, for the construction of a new resort. Slopeside condos were planned, along with Great Camps, and it was hoped that the ski area could reopen by the 2006–07 season. However, due to many permitting issues and eventual lawsuits, the development was put on hold.

In 2009, Jim LaValley, Michael Foxman and Tom Lawson came up with the idea to form a volunteer group to reopen the ski area while the Adirondack Club Resort (ACR) went through the permitting process. The group was called ARISE (Adirondack Residents Intent on Saving our Economy). The goal was to make the ski area viable again to show that the ACR project could work, as well as to bring skiing back to Tupper Lake for residents and visitors alike. They were not directly associated with ACR but were able to lease the ski area for a very nominal rate. At first, they considered just opening the T-bar and a handful of trails, but former owner Peter Day advised that the T-bar was likely too far gone and suggested they take a look at restoring Chair 2. This proved to be the best option, and on September 2, 2009, Cliff Lemaire began inspecting the chairlift.

William "Steve" Stevenson, who had previously worked at Whiteface Mountain, was brought in to help organize the reopening. He drew up an organizational plan for the mountain and coordinated the efforts of community members. News of the reopening traveled fast among Big Tupper residents, with many volunteering to come up to the mountain to clear trails served by Chair 2 (other trails were left as is), clean up a portion of the lodge (which had been vandalized) and get the lift back up and operating. Zach White, who was the former manager at Titus Mountain, was able to recondition the lifts and make them operational again. The Mitey Mite was also in good enough shape to be operated. A groomer was obtained from Sugarbush to keep the trails in good condition. The snowmaking system was in too rough of a shape to be operated, and ARISE did not have the funding needed to operate it, being a mostly volunteer operation. Former ski patrollers came back to the mountain and reorganized themselves.

After much effort, On December 29, 2009, Big Tupper's Chair 2 took its first passengers to the top of its trails. Skiers were once again able to enjoy some of Big Tupper's trails. For that inaugural season, the area was open on Fridays and weekends, with lift tickets at just fifteen dollars, among the lowest rates in the state. While the area offered only basic amenities, local residents and visitors were thrilled to have their area back. The mountain's website and Facebook groups were filled with stories of how happy everybody was to have the area back in operation.

Over the next two seasons, incremental progress continued. Chair 3 was reopened for the 2010–11 season, allowing for summit access, and

The author enjoyed skiing at Big Tupper on January 22, 2010, a short time after its reopening. This view shows the bottom of Chair 1 on the Sluice Way trail. In the background is the base lodge, Sugar Loaf and Tupper Lake.

additional trails were cleared of growth. Chair 1 and the T-bar were too far gone to be restored with the budget available.

After the 2011–12 season, the progress of ACR had ground to a halt. Although it had received Adirondack Park Agency approval (10–1) to begin the development of the resort, the Sierra Club and Protect the Adirondacks, along with some local residents, had filed an Article 78 lawsuit to stop the project. With these delays, ARISE made the decision not to open the ski area for the 2012–13 season. It seemed that, once again, the promise of Big Tupper was not going to happen.

But the ski area did not lie empty for that season. Although inaccessible for skiers, it was the site for the filming of several scenes for the 2014 *Teenage Mutant Ninja Turtles* movie. The directors wanted a secure location with a former ski area, and Big Tupper filled that order. The revenue generated by the filming provided a good nest egg that was given to ARISE to reopen the area for the 2013–14 season. Inconsistent snowfall allowed for only seventeen days of operation, but once again, Big Tupper was open for business.

Chair 2, originally from Dutchess Mountain in the Hudson Valley, is seen in this 2010 view from the Lift Line Trail. This is Big Tupper's second double chairlift and serves a variety of terrain.

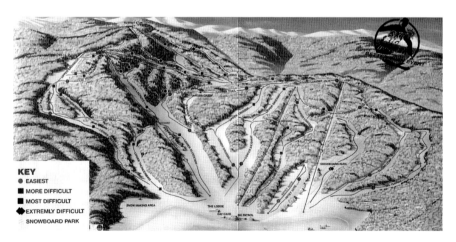

The 1998–99 season was the last one until it reopened in 2009. This trail map shows the extent of the lifts and trails at that time. While Chair 1 and the T-bar are no longer operational, Chair 2 and Chair 3 now provide access to the full mountain. A Mitey Mite lift serves the beginner area. Almost all trails have been restored, although a few have yet to be cleared.

On July 3, 2014, the New York State Supreme Court Appellate Division rebuked the Article 78 challenge, which now allows the ACR project to move forward. Leilani Ulrich of the APA released a statement saying that the project would be "transforming" for the community. Governor Andrew Cuomo praised the project as well and believes it will provide jobs and opportunities for the area.

ARISE fully expects to operate Big Tupper for the 2014–15 and will then pass the baton to the ACR. At the time of this writing, the exact plans for further renovation and expansion of Big Tupper have not been announced, but the future now appears brighter than it has for a long time for the ski area and community. As part of the approval process, ACR agreed to always allow public skiing so the ski area itself will not become a private resort. None of this would have been possible without the support of ARISE and volunteers who worked hard to save their ski area.

Visiting the Area

Big Tupper offers a wide variety of ski terrain, from novices to experts, on interesting and scenic trails. Two chairlifts and a Mitey Mite operate, giving skiers an over 1,100-foot vertical drop. To learn more about Big Tupper, including hours of operation and directions, please visit its website, www.skibigtupper.org, or its Facebook page, at www.facebook.com/skibigtupper.

OTIS MOUNTAIN

Elizabethtown, New York

1965–1970, 1972–1979, 1995–present

Otis Mountain in Elizabethtown was a community ski area that operated from 1965 to 1979, when a lack of snowfall resulted in the area closing. It sat vacant until 1995, when Jeff Allott was able to reopen the ski area on a semi-private basis. Today, the area still operates as a semi-private facility, but there is hope that it will someday be a co-operative area, fully open to the public.

A snowy view from the main slope at Otis Mountain in the late 1960s. Note the new ski lodge at the bottom of the area. *Courtesy of Jeff Allott.*

After the Elizabethtown Ski Center closed in 1959, the land was abandoned, and it seemed as if the dream of a ski area on the mountain had come to an end. However, just five years later, local residents once again brought up the idea of opening a ski area on the site. By December 1964, a bond vote for the $80,000 project was put up before the voters but failed due to a more important hospital referendum. Undaunted, volunteers spent their own time and money and quickly built a 1,200-foot-long rope tow on one of the former ski slopes. This was supported by the Elizabethtown Ski Associates, with a new corporation, the Otis Mountain Ski Corporation, to take over the actual operation. Lights for night skiing were also installed. All of this was completed in time for a January 30, 1965 opening.

The restored area quickly gained support, with many townspeople glad to see skiing back. Residents were hopeful that it would provide a fun and healthy activity for young people and keep them out of trouble in the winter.

For the following fall, the proposal to bond the town to expand the center was considered but ultimately withdrawn. The idea of the town getting into the ski business had been a radioactive topic amongst town politicians. Even without government support, the corporation worked hard to improve the mountain over the next few years. In 1967, a new clubhouse with sitting

Children and new skiers frequently used the rope tow at Otis Mountain in the 1970s. It still operates today as the main lift. *By Bob Harsh, courtesy of Jeff Allott.*

A young skier catches a ride on the T-bar at Otis Mountain in the 1970s. The lift was nearly 1,600 feet in length and provided skiers a run of 375 feet. Originally from Windham Mountain, the lift was installed at Otis in 1970. *By Bob Harsh, courtesy of Jeff Allott.*

areas, a kitchen and a snack bar was built at the foot of the slopes and provided a comfortable setting for skiers to take a break.

With the area growing, sights were set on expanding the mountain. By 1970, the corporation had trouble paying its bills and asked Herb and Jane Hildebrandt to purchase the ski area. They did so and quickly purchased a used T-bar that had operated at Windham Mountain in the Catskills. The total cost for the lift, transportation and installation totaled more than $7,000, a huge expense for the Hildebrandts. They had to postpone opening the mountain for two years, until 1972, to have time to recover their losses. Once reopened, the ski area expanded in size to include a beginner slope with an associated rope tow, a new slope served by the 1,600-foot-long T-bar and half a mile of twisting trail through the woods.

The Hildebrandts valiantly operated the ski area until 1979. It was a popular and affordable location for nearby families who could not afford the higher prices of larger ski areas such as Whiteface. Many locals also enjoyed night skiing, which was not common at other areas in the Adirondacks.

Jeff Allott, the present owner of Otis Mountain, shares his memories of this decade:

> The '70s were a great time in Otis Mountains history in that the snow was abundant and attendance was high. The mountain was run by Herb and Jane Hildebrandt, a fantastic couple who loved the hill and the kids that skied there, but never really skied themselves. This was truly and obviously a labor of love for them. I recall that it was a community-wide project to get the hill to where it was, too, with many families involved in the process. People would get "shares" in exchange for their efforts, and I believe over one hundred were issued over the years. They did not amount to having any value in the end but were proudly passed between generations.
>
> There was a fully functional lodge with bathrooms, a first aid room, a small food counter and a large wood stove. Large picture windows looked out over the hill, and I can always remember the parking lots being full. All of the local schools used Otis for their ski programs at that time, and I recall quite a few school buses there on weekends. There were two main hills, a T-bar, a rope row and numerous steep and tight trails snaking down the sides. We also had Wednesday Night Skiing through that decade, and it would be announced over the PA system at school every Wednesday morning during the winter. Back then, almost everyone skied at some level, and there was always excitement about that event. I was in my teens through that

period, and I literally grew up on the hill. I remember the night skiing as being magical and could not wait until Wednesday night each week. It was the ultimate high school mixer, where kids from all of the surrounding schools showed up to socialize and show off. That was when skiing in jeans was cool, by the way!

It was also a great place to work during those times, and a few of us were lucky enough to get a job there. Throughout that period, I did every job imaginable, from serving lifts, to making hot dogs, to teaching skiing, and was part of the first "official" ski patrol there with my dad. Needless to say, it was a big part of my life at that time. I also remember the parking and road in as being especially muddy in the spring, and getting cars and buses out at the end of a warm day was a messy and extended event. I left the area in 1977 to travel (it was also the glory days to be a ski bum) and lost touch with Otis for a few years.

The 1979–80 season was full of anticipation for many areas in the northern Adirondacks like Otis, as the Winter Olympics would be taking place in Lake Placid. However, that was the start of two back-to-back snowless seasons. Virtually no snow fell through the end of February. This hit the area hard with severe losses, which were "very discouraging" to the Hildebrandts. These losses forced them to close the ski area.

Another attempt was made a few years later to reopen the mountain. According to Allott:

Andy McCabe, approached the town board in 1982 (I think) with the idea of firing it up again as a town effort. A great deal of work went in to getting the hill back up to code and clearing the trails that had grown in very quickly. The lodge was restored, the hill insured and everything was ready, but it never snowed that year, and Otis went back to sleep once again.

It seemed as if Otis would be gone for good, but Allott had other plans. He went on to purchase the area and reopen it as a semi-private area. Here is how he did it:

I would regularly run into Herb or Jane and always promise that I would someday get the hill running again. More years went by, and Herb passed away. I started my own little manufacturing company (yes we did some ski and snowboard products) with a close friend and had the opportunity to move my business back to the Adirondacks in 1994, continuing to make

Jane Hildebrandt (right), the former co-owner of Otis Mountain, visited the ski area in 2006, and is pictured here with Jeff Allott's son Zach. Jane and her late husband, Herb, operated Otis for nearly a decade. *Courtesy of Jeff Allott.*

the same promise to Jane every time I ran into her. The Otis property had been listed for sale for many years but had fallen into disrepair, and there was never much interest in it. I remember getting a panicked call from Jane in 1995 because someone had shown some interest in the property, and she was afraid that I would never get the chance to reopen the hill. I barely had two nickels to rub together at the time but was able to pull in two friends and co-workers and find someone willing to loan us the money. It was summer, and we ran the hill that winter. I do not know how we pulled that off, but we have been running every winter ever since.

Since 1995, the hill has been run as a "private" ski slope for extended friends and family, and quite a few kids learned to ski during that time. There was no cost to ski there, and people would bring food as a gesture of thanks and it turned in to quite an event each weekend there was snow. The last twenty years went by really quickly, and I am now looking to move to the next step and possibly create a co-op that would allow us to open the hill to more people and possibly create a biking and hiking trail system.

Today, Otis continues to operate on a limited basis, with one rope tow and two open slopes, though one is used more frequently than the other as it is next to the tow. The T-bar slope is partially overgrown but is available

Jeff Allott had to repair the rope tow in 1995, which had sat unused for sixteen years. A used 1950s boat engine was installed to power the lift. *Courtesy of Jeff Allott.*

The rope tow at Otis Mountain was not always reliable once it reopened in the 1990s—in this example, once the lift had broken down, a Sno-Cat was used to haul skiers to the top using an attached rope. *Courtesy of Jeff Allott.*

The Hall T-bar at Otis Mountain no longer operates, but the engine house and lift towers still stand. It makes for a "lost area within an open area."

for those who wish to hike to the top. The T-bar was partially removed, but the towers are still standing, along with the engine house. As Allott alluded to, there are hopes one day to expand the operation to include being open to the public.

Visiting the Area

The ski area is open sporadically to the public each winter for the Backcountry Ski Festival, and in the fall it hosts the Otis Mountain Getdown Music Festival. To learn more about these events, please visit www.otismountain.com.

VII

Proposed Ski Areas of the Northern Adirondacks

Three ski areas were seriously proposed but never developed in the Adirondacks. Two of them, McKenzie Mountain and Blue Ridge, would have been amongst the largest ski areas in the state and in the northeastern corner of the country. Both would have been developed on state land and would have required constitutional amendments for their development. McKenzie never made it past the proposal stage, while Blue Ridge failed at the ballot box. Apple Valley never got off the ground due to a landowner refusing to sell his land for the project.

It is hard to know what the ski scene would have been like in the northern Adirondacks had even one of the proposed areas been built. The presence of more significant ski areas operated by the state could have brought more attention to the area as a serious ski destination. On the other hand, opponents claimed that these developments would have seriously hurt private ski areas that did not have the luxury of using state funds.

In addition to these three areas, some ski areas with plans to become much larger were partially built but never achieved their full potential, including Jenkins Mountain in Paul Smiths and Lowenberg in Dannemora, which can be read about in their sections in chapters two and four, respectively.

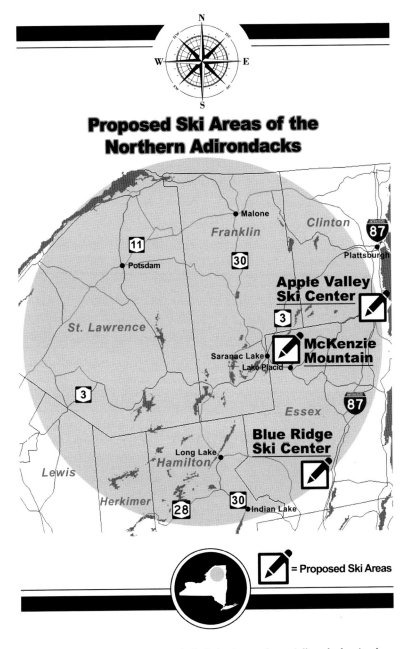

Three proposed ski areas were nearly built in the northern Adirondacks: Apple Valley in Keeseville, Blue Ridge in North Hudson/Schroon Lake and McKenzie Mountain in North Elba. *Courtesy of Brandon Capasso.*

APPLE VALLEY SKI CENTER ON BIGELOW MOUNTAIN

Keeseville, New York

Proposed 1960–1966

The smallest of the seriously proposed ski areas, Apple Valley Ski Center was to have been built on Bigelow Mountain in Keeseville in the 1960s. It was to have been operated by the Keeseville Kiwanis as a community ski area, geared toward families. The name Apple Valley was selected as homage to the nearby orchards of the area, and indeed, the base of the ski area would have been in one of those orchards. After six years of planning and false starts, the concept was abandoned in 1966.

The Keeseville Kiwanis, seeing the explosion of ski areas in the northern Adirondacks, wanted to develop a ski center of their own. Out of all the nearby hills and mountains, the 1,600-foot-tall Bigelow Mountain, four miles to the south of Keeseville, was selected in 1959. During the following winter, snow surveys were taken, and potential trails were laid out. Ron McKenzie, the ski expert from Lake Placid, was brought in as a consultant and gave his approval. Roy Kennedy was appointed the head of the Ski Development Committee. Other Kiwanis members Wilfred Cohen, Alban Fitzpatrick, Richard Smith, Joseph Silverman, Gregory Adams and Robert Laundree were also appointed to the committee.

The original plan, announced in 1960, was $50,000 to build a 2,200-foot-long T-bar lift on a 500-foot vertical drop on the north slope of Bigelow. A T-bar was considered and not a rope tow due to the sometimes-dangerous reputation of the tows. Trails of up to three-quarters of a mile long were planned, with the goal of keeping them relatively narrow to protect the forest. The area would be the perfect family- or mid-sized mountain, with more features than a short, open-slope rope tow area but fewer than developments like Whiteface.

Portions of the mountain were owned by committee member Alban Fitzpatrick, who would sell the land to the Kiwanis for well below its value. J.B. Mace, who would allow the use of his land if needed, owned another piece of property.

Momentum continued to grow, and by March 1961, the project was "now a certainty." Plans were made to clear slopes, add a parking lot and renovate apple barns at the base into a lodge for that summer. Bonds were sold, and it looked like there would be enough financing to move the project forward. In April 1961, Walter Prager, the former Dartmouth ski coach, now living in Wilmington, visited the area and made recommendations about how to develop the ski area. In August, Jack Wikoff of Lake Placid (who had developed Kobl Mountain) was also consulted on its development.

No work was performed on the mountain that summer, as planned, or the following year either. During this time, the $50,000 project started to expand in scope, with a chairlift now planned. In addition, the expected arrival of the Adirondack Northway around the side of the ski area would make the area the first to be seen by Canadians traveling south, increasing its potential value. The cost soon rose to as high as $250,000. Seeing the potential growth, the landowner of where the bottom of the ski area was to be built refused to sell the land unless he received a very high price for it.

The project quickly ground to a halt. An attempt at its revival in 1966 also failed. Had it actually been built, it would have been one of the more easily accessible ski areas in the Adirondacks, as Exit 34 on the Northway was built only about one mile away from mountain.

McKenzie Mountain

North Elba, New York

Proposed 1954–1956

In 1954, local Lake Placid and Saranac Lake skiers and business leaders sought to develop a ski area close to their respective villages. Local areas were on the small side, and Marble Mountain, the largest at the time in the northern Adirondacks, was a considerable distance away. Plans began to form to develop a center on McKenzie Mountain, a nearby mountain where vertical drops of over two thousand feet were possible. In addition, a development here was thought to be able to lure the Olympics back to Lake Placid for 1960.

In early 1955, a new group, the Lake Placid–Saranac Lake Joint Committee for the Development of Mount McKenzie, was formed to develop the next steps. Founding members included Ron MacKenzie and Thomas Cantwell. Snow measurements taken proved that deep snows were consistent during the winter. A proposal was made, with three chairlifts to the north peak of Mount McKenzie, an octagon-shaped glass building at the summit and a new access road from near the Whiteface Inn. A potential cost of $2 million was estimated for the project, which would directly compete against larger ski areas in New England.

By 1957, momentum had grown, and in February, a large model of the potential ski area, complete with real snow, was sent to Albany so that Governor Harriman could be directly lobbied. This was not successful, and shortly afterward the plan stalled. It is likely that the development of Whiteface Mountain shortly thereafter stymied the project. The mountain later became part of the McKenzie Wilderness Area.

Several hiking trails are available to explore the mountain, with directions available at www.lakeplacid.com/do/hiking/mckenzie-mountain.

BLUE RIDGE SKI CENTER ON HOFFMAN MOUNTAIN

North Hudson and Schroon Lake, New York

Proposed 1963–1967

Had it been developed, the Blue Ridge Ski Center on Hoffman Mountain would have been one of the most extensive ski areas in New York State. Years of planning went into its development, from 1963 until 1967, from local business groups to legislators. The state constitutional amendment required to build the area was soundly defeated in November 1967 and was never revived.

In the 1960s, ski areas in New England, especially Vermont, were rapidly developing. Meanwhile, in New York, only a few ski areas of significant size—including Whiteface and the brand-new Gore Mountain in the Adirondacks, along with Catskill areas Windham, Belleayre and Hunter—had been developed. Many skiers were opting to leave the state and instead enjoy the larger offerings in nearby Vermont.

To help remedy this situation, a group of mostly Essex County local business owners and other concerned citizens formed a group that would petition the state to build a ski area on Hoffman Mountain, in North Hudson and Schroon Lake. The mountain was mostly on Forever Wild land and would need a constitutional amendment if it was to be developed.

From 1963 until 1966, the mountain was studied to confirm its feasibility of hosting a ski area. With a peak elevation of 3,700 feet, it would be taller

A painting of the proposed Blue Ridge Ski Center was made by Ella Tyrrell, a supporter of the project. Her vision of the ski area included a lodge overlooking the slopes, filled with happy skiers. *By Ella Tyrrell, courtesy of Roger Friedman.*

than almost all other ski areas in the state. Various bowls would provide all levels of skiing, including a novice trail from the top. Vertical drops of over 2,000 feet were possible. Notable expert Otto Schniebs, along with Moe Friedman, took snow surveys and studies and determined that the mountain was perfect for a ski area. Indeed, there was so much snow that they had to turn around before reaching the summit. A major lift such as a gondola was proposed, along with chairlifts on West and East Peaked Hill, which would allow for trails up to two miles in length.

Convincing the legislature was another matter. In New York, it takes two consecutive years of both the state senate and assembly to pass an amendment. Following this, it would need to be submitted to voters, who had the final say. The group of local leaders, led by Moe Friedman of Schroon Lake, pushed the legislature hard to pass the bills in 1965, but it did not pass the assembly. In the following year, they convinced more local town boards to approve the proposal to gain support. This paid off in 1966 and 1967, when both branches passed what would be called

Governor Nelson Rockefeller, on the right, meets with Moe and Janet Friedman of Schroon Lake to lend his support to the project and look at a model of the ski area. Despite the governor's support, Amendment Two to approve the Blue Ridge Ski Center was handily defeated. *Courtesy of Roger Friedman.*

Amendment Two. Its wording for a public vote on November 9, 1967, was as follows:

> *Form of Submission of Proposed Amendment Number Two—Blue Ridge Ski Center—Shall the proposed amendment to Article fourteen, Section one, of the Constitution, permitting the State to construct and maintain not more than thirty miles of ski trails, thirty to eighty feet wide, together with appurtenances thereto, on forest preserve land on the north and east slopes of Hoffman, Blue Ridge, and Peaked Hill Mountains in Essex County be approved?*

Once the vote was scheduled, however, opposition from groups and towns across the state ensued. Editorials (mainly from regions away from Essex County) were written in many newspapers decrying the proposal. Opponents felt that the state was already in too deep in the ski business, having just opened Gore Mountain and already operating Whiteface Mountain. Other ski areas protested as well, as they were struggling to obtain funds for expansions and complained that they could not compete against a state-funded venture.

Support groups counteracted these claims, stating that the state needed more areas to compete against other states and that the area would boost tourism across a wide region, putting the Adirondacks on the map. They also stated that since the state owned almost all of the suitable large mountains for development, this would be the only way to build a large-scale facility. Governor Nelson Rockefeller also made a plea for the development with his full support.

On November 9, 1967, voters went to the polls. Amendment Two was soundly defeated, passing only in the towns within a thirty-mile radius of the ski area. In some locations, such as Tupper Lake, the proposal was defeated nine to one. Local leaders were dismayed that all of their work to build this ski area was in vain and never tried to revive the proposal.

There is no telling what the impact of this large ski area would have been on the Adirondacks. Its proximity to the Northway certainly would have made it very accessible, placing the area about five hours north of New York City with all-highway access. Canadians also would have been able to easily reach the area. One can envision that the Blue Ridge Ski Center would have been a huge boon for the eastern Adirondacks but would also have potential adversely affected smaller ski areas that could not compete.

VIII

Operating Ski Areas of the Northern Adirondacks

Despite the loss of forty-seven ski areas, several opportunities still exist for skiers across the northern Adirondacks. The operating ski areas of the northern Adirondacks include ski areas for everybody—from experts seeking Olympic thrills at Whiteface, to strong community ski areas like Mount Pisgah, to family-operated Titus Mountain, to not-for-profit areas like Beartown.

Each of these areas is critical to the continuation of the sport across the northern Adirondacks. Besides offering exciting outdoor recreational opportunities, these ski areas teach thousands the sport, ensuring its survival. The author implores you to check out every single one of these areas—you will be glad you did!

This chapter provides information on each of these areas, including directions, trail and lift information and websites. The author is also aware of a few completely private ski areas in the region, but these are not listed in order to protect the privacy of their owners. At the Olympic Jumping Complex in Lake Placid, a chairlift operates for jumpers during competitions and for sightseers in the summer, but it is not considered an alpine ski area.

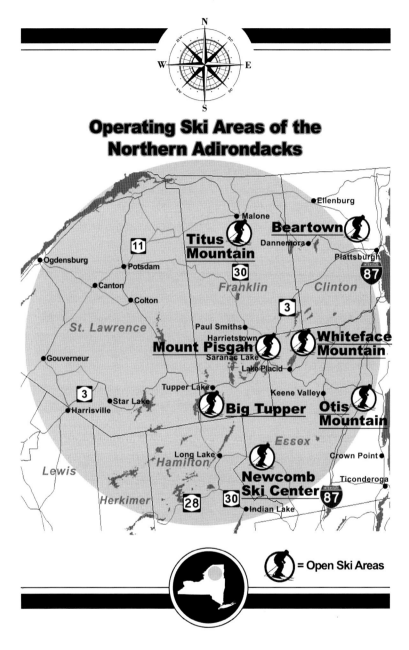

Out of the fifty-four ski areas that once operated in the northern Adirondacks, only seven still operate. Each of these areas is unique and fills a particular niche, from racing runs used in the Olympics at Whiteface to family-friendly terrain at Mount Pisgah. *Courtesy of Brandon Capasso.*

OTIS MOUNTAIN

Lobdell Road, Elizabethtown, NY 12932

TRAILS: 2, plus glades
LIFT-SERVED VERTICAL DROP: 120 feet
HIKE-TO-TERRAIN VERTICAL DROP: 325 feet
LIFTS: 1 rope tow
NIGHT SKIING: Yes
WEBSITE: www.otismountain.com

For more information on Otis Mountain, please see its section in chapter six.

TITUS MOUNTAIN

215 Johnson Road, Malone, NY 12953

TRAILS: 42
VERTICAL DROP: 1,200 feet
LIFTS: 10—2 triples, 6 doubles, 2 handle tows
NIGHT SKIING: Yes
WEBSITE: www.titusmountain.com
PHONE: 800-848-8766

Formerly known as Moon Valley, Titus Mountain is the second largest ski area in the northern Adirondacks and offers a surprising variety of skiing. Five mountain faces are available to ski, each with its own lift(s), with scenic trails and glades for all abilities. It is also the widest ski area in the region—nearly two miles wide! In recent years, the owners, the Monette family of Malone, have made many improvements, adding additional trails, chutes and glades; renovating the lodge; adding snowmaking (covering 70 percent of terrain); and hosting more events. Ticket rates are affordable, and a strong ski school program is available. For non-skiers, a tubing park provides downhill thrills.

Newcomb Ski Slope/Goodnow Ski Area

*0.7 miles south on Goodnow Flow Road,
from intersection of Pine Tree Road and Goodnow Flow Road,
Newcomb, NY 12852*

Trails: 1 wide beginner-intermediate main slope on skier's right of the T-bar, 1 intermediate chute on skier's left of the T-bar, 1 intermediate woods trail
Vertical Drop: 180 feet
Lifts: 1 T-bar with midstation
Night Skiing: No
Website: www.newcombny.com
Phone: 518-582-4621

A town-funded and town-supported ski area, the Newcomb Ski Slope (sometimes known as the Goodnow Ski Area) features uncrowded, pleasurable skiing with spectacular views of the High Peak region to the north. A T-bar provides access to three downhill routes, including a wide-open slope and a fun, twisting woods trail. There is no snowmaking, but natural snowfall is usually plentiful, and the trails are groomed. A warming hut is available, but there is no food service. While there is no cost to use the area, the author reccomends that visitors support local stores/restaurants whose taxes help pay for the operation.

Mount Pisgah Veteran's Memorial Ski Center

92 Mount Pisgah Lane, Saranac Lake, NY 12983

Trails: 15 acres, 1 large beginner-intermediate slope with several chutes, side trails and glades
Vertical Drop: 329 feet
Lifts: 1 T-bar, 1 tubing lift
Night Skiing: Yes
Website: www.saranaclakeny.gov/pisgah
Phone: 518-891-0970

Mount Pisgah is a textbook example of what can happen when a community fully supports a local ski area. Today, Pisgah is thriving as a completely modernized ski center with something to offer for everybody. Owned and operated by the Village of Saranac Lake, with strong support from the Friends of Mount Pisgah, the area has made tremendous improvements in the last several years. These include a brand-new T-bar lift, a modern snowmaking system, a brand-new lodge with expansive views of the slope and snack bar and a new tubing park. None of this could have been accomplished without the hard work of volunteers and the support of the village.

For skiing, a new T-bar takes skiers to the top of the hill, where they can enjoy a variety of downhill runs, from a wide-open slope to many chutes and backcountry glades with beautiful views. The main slope features beginner and intermediate aspects with occasional quick dips in the terrain to keep it interesting. The glades section is especially popular with children, who enjoy exploring its terrain. Ticket prices are very affordable, and night skiing is available. Cross-country skiers and snowshoers can enjoy three and a half kilometers of trails. If you cannot ski Mount Pisgah in person, please check out its webcam on the ski area link to watch the action from home.

BIG TUPPER

End of Ski Tow Road, Tupper Lake, NY 12986

TRAILS: 25
VERTICAL DROP: 1,151 feet
LIFTS: 2 doubles, 1 Mitey Mite
NIGHT SKIING: No
WEBSITE: www.skibigtupper.org
PHONE: 518-359-3730

For more information on Big Tupper, please see its section in chapter six.

Beartown

Beartown Road, West Chazy, NY 12992

Trails: 9
Vertical Drop: 130 feet
Lifts: 1 T-bar, 1 Pomalift
Night Skiing: Yes
Website: www.skibeartown.com
Phone: 518-561-3938

A not-for-profit ski area supported by members and volunteers, Beartown offers a wide variety of features for winter sports enthusiasts. Despite a vertical drop of only 130 feet, it offers nine beginner- to low-intermediate-level trails, perfect for families and those learning the sport. From the summit, one can see Lake Champlain and Vermont in the distance. Miles of cross-country ski and snowshoe trails are also available. The ski area offers lessons, and the Beartown Ski Team teaches children the art and fun of skiing racing in an enjoyable environment. Skiers can refuel at the snack bar inside the cozy base lodge that overlooks the slopes. Beartown is a true representation of what many former ski areas used to offer: family-friendly skiing in a wonderful setting.

Whiteface Mountain

5021 Route 86, Wilmington, NY 12997

Trails: 87
Lift-Served Vertical Drop: 3,166 feet
Hike-to-Terrain Vertical Drop: 3,430 feet
Lifts: 11—1 gondola, 1 high-speed quad, 1 fixed-grip quad, 5 doubles, 2 triples, 1 carpet
Night Skiing: No
Website: www.whiteface.com
Phone: 877-SKIFACE

Whiteface, "The Olympic Mountain," features the tallest vertical drop of any ski area east of the Mississippi River. Operated by ORDA (the Olympic

Regional Development Authority), the ski area has all the features of a modern resort, except slopeside lodging. Twenty-two miles of ski trails, from novice to expert, challenge all abilities. The 1980 Winter Olympics skiing events were held at the mountain, and skiers today can enjoy those same routes raced by world-class athletes. In the last few years, the Lookout Mountain area was developed with a new lift and several trails; its summit is located just a short distance from the former Upper Mountain area of the lost Marble Mountain. For skiers looking for a serious challenge, the Slides typically open in late winter and are accessible via a hike from the top of the Summit Quad.

Afterword

The northern Adirondacks have seen the loss of forty-seven ski areas—a number significantly higher than most would have guessed. They ranged from small community areas that taught locals to ski, to college and university ski areas that were used by students, to complete resorts that offered weeklong ski vacations. Almost all were places of employment for local residents and places to recreate with friends and family. Some of the larger areas attracted skiers from out of town who came and spent their money on local businesses and restaurants.

Losing so many of these areas has been hard on the region. Many of those interviewed in the book lament that that young people will not have the same opportunities that they had. A good number of these ski areas had the potential to be permanent fixtures in their communities, but many factors, often outside the control of the individual ski area, intervened to prevent this from occurring.

Although so many areas have been lost, there remain several opportunities for a wonderful experience at a smaller or family-run ski area. Most of the existing ski areas are run by families, towns or not-for-profit groups and continue the strong tradition of the many areas that came before them. It is critical to continue to support these ski areas—and the author recommends that readers visit them.

The time is now to continue to preserve the history of these areas. Almost all of the lost areas are fading away and, in a few decades, will disappear from the landscape completely. These areas can be preserved in myriad ways—from donating materials to local historical societies and museums, sharing your memories with your family and posting your experiences and photographs electronically.

NELSAP.org, operated by the author, is a vast repository of information pertaining to lost ski areas. Through the website, visitors can contribute their information and photos to share with the world. A companion Facebook page, www.facebook.com/LostSkiAreasoftheNorthernAdirondacks, is another online source to contribute materials and have discussions with fellow ski history enthusiasts.

The author hopes that you have enjoyed your tour of the many ski areas that no longer exist and that their impacts will not be forgotten.

Bibliography

Adirondack Daily Enterprise (Saranac Lake, NY), February 1950–April 2002.

Adirondack Record–Elizabethtown Post (Elizabethtown, NY), July 1966–January 1967.

Adler, Allen. *New England & Thereabouts—A Ski Tracing.* Barton, VT: Netco Press, 1985.

Allen, John, and Ekkehart Ulmrich. "The Man Who Started It All: Otto Schniebs." *Skiing Heritage Journal,* Autumn 1996.

A.T. Eye (Canton, NY), May 1960.

Au Sable Fords Record-Post (Au Sable, NY), December 1936–February 1967.

Buxton, John. *Eastern Ski Slopes.* Greenwich, CT: John S. Herold, Inc., 1964.

Canton Commercial Advertiser (Canton, NY), December 1941–Jan 1943.

Chateaugay Record (Chateaugay, NY), December 1945–August 1957.

Clarkson Integrator (Potsdam, NY), March 1950–October 1991.

Courier and Freeman (Potsdam, NY), August 1967–December 1989.

Elkins, Frank. *The Complete Ski Guide.* New York: Doubleday, Doran & Company, Inc., 1940.

Federal Writer's Project. *Skiing in the East: The Best Ski Trails and How to Get There.* New York: M. Barrows & Company, 1939.

Fort Covington Sun (Fort Covington, NY), November 1967

Hill News (Canton, NY), St. Lawrence University, February 1936–February 2006.

Journal and Republican (Lowville, NY), March 1995.

Lake Placid News (Lake Placid, NY), January 1936–January 2008.

Landman, Joan, and David Landman. *Where to Ski*. Boston: Houghton Mifflin Company, 1949.

Massena New York Observer (Massena, NY), October 1960–December 1972.

National Parks Service. "Historic American Engineering Record— Plattsburgh Air Force Base." Report, 2000. http://lcweb2.loc.gov/pnp/ habshaer/ny/ny1800/ny1864/data/ny1864data.pdf.

North Country Catholic (Ogdensburg, NY), August 1965.

Northern Light (Plattsburgh, NY), SUNY Plattsburgh, February 1949.

Ogdensburg Journal (Ogdensburg, NY), March 1940–December 1989.

Pain, William. *The American Ski Directory*. New York: Permabooks, 1961.

Plattsburgh Daily Press (Plattsburgh, NY), January 1938.

Plattsburgh Daily Republican (NY), February 1942.

Plattsburgh Press-Republican (Plattsburgh, NY), December 1946–March 1991

Sandy Creek News (Sandy Creek, NY), December 1967.

Schenectady Gazette (Schenectady, NY), March 1958.

Ski New York Brochures, 1939–1970.

Ski New York Guidebooks, 1949–1953.

Ticonderoga Sentinel (Ticonderoga, NY), February 1956–November 1967.

Times Record (Troy, NY), February 1941.

Times Union (Albany, NY), July 3, 2014.

Tribune-Press (Gouverneur, NY), September 1950–September 1998.

Tupper Lake Free Press (Tupper Lake, NY), April 1936–July 2014.

U.S. Ski and Snowboard Hall of Fame and Museum. "Otto Schneibs." http://www.skihall.com/index.php?_a=document&doc_id=11&id=297.

Van de Water, Peter E. Report on St. Lawrence University Snow Bowl. St. Lawrence University, April 1974.

Watertown Daily Times (Watertown, NY), September 1966–November 1976.

About the Author

Jeremy Davis is a passionate skier and has enjoyed exploring skiing history from the moment he learned how to ski. A 2000 graduate from Lyndon State College in Vermont, he is an operations manager/ meteorologist at Weather Routing Inc., in Glens Falls, New York, where he provides professional weather forecasts to marine clients worldwide. Jeremy has served on the New England Ski Museum's board of directors since 2000. His website, the New England/Northeast Lost Ski Areas Project (www.nelsap.org), has been in operation since 1998 and, in 2009, won the prestigious Cyber Award for best ski history website from the International Ski History  Association. He is the author of three additional books, *Lost Ski Areas of the White Mountains* (2008), *Lost Ski Areas of Southern Vermont* (2010) and *Lost Ski Areas of the Southern Adirondacks* (2012), which won the International Ski History Association's Skade Award for Outstanding Regional Ski History. Jeremy is a member of Ski Venture in Glenville, New York, one of the oldest surviving ski clubs that still operates a rope tow–only ski area. He resides just outside the Adirondacks near Saratoga Springs, New York.

Visit us at
www.historypress.net
....
This title is also available as an e-book